JOHN EDGAR WIDEMAN

A Study of the Short Fiction

Also available in Twayne's Studies in Short Fiction Series

Twayne publishes studies of all major short-story writers worldwide. For a complete list, contact the Publisher directly.

Twayne's Studies in Short Fiction

Gary Scharnhorst and Eric Haralson
General Editors

JOHN EDGAR WIDEMAN.
Courtesy News Office.

JOHN EDGAR WIDEMAN
A Study of the Short Fiction

Keith E. Byerman
Indiana State University

TWAYNE PUBLISHERS

New York

Twayne's Studies in Short Fiction, No. 70

Twayne Publishers

1633 Broadway
New York, NY 10019

Library of Congress Cataloging-in-Publication Data
Byerman, Keith Eldon, 1948–
    John Edgar Wideman : a study of the short fiction / Keith E.
Byerman.
       p.   cm. — (Twayne's studies in short fiction ; no. 70)
    Includes bibliographical references and index.
    ISBN 0-8057-0870-7
    1. Wideman, John Edgar—Criticism and interpretation. 2. Afro-
American authors—20th century—Interviews. 3. Homewood
(Pittsburgh, Pa.)—In literature. 4. Wideman, John Edgar—
Interviews. 5. Afro-Americans in literature. 6. Short story.
I. Title. II. Series.
PS3573.I26Z58   1998
813'.54—dc21
                                 97-43160
                                    CIP

Contents

Preface

John Edgar Wideman is one of the most prolific African-American short-fiction writers. He has published more stories than Richard Wright, James Baldwin, or Alice Walker, all of whom are better known. Like them, he has won a number of literary prizes and has received the serious attention of reviewers and literary critics. He has published articles in popular and literary magazines and has been the subject of pieces in *People* and *Esquire* magazines, and his works have been the focus of two books of literary analysis. He has held academic positions in creative writing and African-American Studies at the University of Pennsylvania, the University of Wyoming, and the University of Massachusetts. He has published 14 books of fiction and nonfiction since 1972. Yet for all the productivity and critical attention, he has not achieved the level of recognition of other modern black writers.

The very qualities that make him an important contemporary voice may account in part for this general lack of acknowledgment. Wideman has chosen to place himself in the modernist and postmodernist tradition rather than in the critical realist tradition most commonly associated with black writers. James Coleman has written extensively about Wideman's conscious effort early in his career to write in the modes of T. S. Eliot and William Faulkner.[1] His first novels were filled with wasteland imagery and with characters who lived lives of desperation, whether quiet or not. His particular contribution to the tradition was to locate his narratives in the modern ghetto, with its frustration, anger, and hopelessness. He used stream of consciousness and other modernist techniques to reveal the levels of this despair and impotence. These works were recognized for their craftsmanship, but the very sophistication and alienation expressed in them worked against a large audience.

In the late 1970s, as Wideman has indicated and Coleman and other critics have detailed, he reevaluated his artistic vision. Partly as a result of working with the Black Studies program at the University of Pennsylvania, he began reading and writing about black literature. He also began thinking about the literary value of the Homewood community of Pittsburgh, where he grew up. Stories by and about family members took shape as an alternative to his earlier approach. The history of his family and the community became a saga developed first in the Homewood trilogy—*Damballah* (1981), *Hiding Place* (1981), *Sent for You Yesterday* (1983)—and then in other works of long and short fiction and nonfiction.

The new approach meant a change not only in subject matter but also in technique. He made use of both family stories and the processes of oral storytelling. Further, he incorporated the literal history of himself and the community into his narratives. He made use of the actual names of people, the things that happened to them, and the events of his own life and those of close relatives. In effect he collapsed the distinction between fiction, history, and autobiography. The result might be characterized as black postmodernism. It incorporates the breaking down of discursive boundaries, the self-consciousness of narration, and the skepticism about the relation between fiction and reality that are traits of postmodernist literary practice. But it does so by simultaneously using the associational and digressive methods of folk storytelling. The emphasis is on the representation of ordinary voices that tell the tales of the community and the family. Often set against these voices and their tales is the black intellectual, whose assumptions about truth and value they challenge.

The stories lead to the past and also to contemporary issues. One characteristic of Wideman's method is that he is constantly exploring the connections between past and present. He seeks the recovery of family and social history, not for some antiquarian purpose but in order to illuminate the present. In the *Damballah* stories and elsewhere, the narrative voices reconstruct the past in a way that reveals important values and moral options for contemporary life. In the wasteland that he depicts as the urban African-American landscape, the alternative to despair can be found only in the experiences of those who have gone before and faced even greater difficulties. So the stories of the Wideman and French families become resources for other African Americans.

But there is another, more personal element to the author's work. His brother Robert is in prison for life without parole for participation in a crime in which a killing occurred. Wideman repeatedly refers to the incident and to his brother in both autobiographical and fictional forms. The crime, the imprisonment, and the effects on family members are a constant motif in the fictions. It could even be argued that a primary motivation for the writing is the quest to understand this situation. One question is how two brothers from the same household, faced with the same problems, could have such different fates; one is a lifelong prisoner, whereas the other is a respected academic and writer.

Beyond the immediate circumstance is the larger question of urban deterioration and its effects on young black men. This leads to stories of violence and degradation set in a world where human life seems to have little value. It also leads to narratives about racism, in both its historical and recent manifestations. Wideman often assumes a continuity in the nation's attitudes, from the days of the new republic to yesterday's *New York Times* articles on child abuse. It is because the present is so difficult and because history offers so little reason for optimism that he turns to the tales of endurance and family loyalty.

Wideman uses contemporary techniques of narration in conjunction with traditional African-American storytelling to communicate his vision. Although the two might seem at odds, he locates in them a connection, in, first, a digressive style that permits the introduction of different discourses, and second, in the recovery of voices that are often suppressed. A number of recent writers have brought into literary play voices too often ignored, but Wideman pushes the concept further than most. He uses a dying newborn, prisoners, the insane, and a character named John Edgar Wideman as narrators along with young and old black women and men. In doing so, he highlights the importance of storytelling as a means of understanding reality; it becomes lived experience that matters to the tellers in ways that it cannot in conventional fictional narration. And because these speakers and their subjects are so often ignored or suppressed, it is that much more important that their stories be told. In this sense, the process and the content are closely integrated.

In his emphasis on recovered voices and histories, Wideman refuses to become simplistic or sentimental. The stories focus on the complexities and ambiguities of human experience, wherever it is lived. His family tales are replete with unresolved tensions, conflicting memories, and emotional struggles. One central conflict has to do with father figures and their relationships with their children, especially sons. The father is often either an absence or an incomprehensible presence. Even when he is heroic, as in the case of John French, his very assertiveness is a cause for concern and even fear. In the 1994 autobiographical work *Fatheralong*, Wideman suggests that racism has made it impossible for black fathers to provide a meaningful model of masculine achievement for their sons. In his fiction, he has been dramatizing this point since early in his career. He does so both by telling stories of the fathers in relationship to their sons and by telling stories of sons lost without fathers. The creation and re-creation of family narratives serves in part as a means of providing male ancestors for those sons.

Finally, Wideman's language is an important part of his method. He works hard to grant authenticity to the voices of his storytellers. He uses the violent language of the streets, the spiritual one of the women of the church, the analytical one of black intellectuals and artists, and the bittersweet one of bluesmen. At the same time, he interweaves an alternately meditative and urgent voice much like his own. This voice is used often in passages of free indirect discourse or interior monologue or in narrative exposition. The effect is that very little in his stories can be labeled as objective or neutral in its articulation. The texts have an intensity and insistence that run counter to the cool irony of much contemporary fiction.

John Edgar Wideman uses the devices of modernism and postmodernism not to position himself as an ontological or epistemological skeptic but rather to engage the world as fully as possible. He produces an "urgent" fiction that demands that readers pay attention to the troubled and often desperate voices of the African-American community. By blending past and present, distinct modes of discourse, and different narrative techniques, Wideman brings tradition to bear on contemporary concerns and characters. He in effect constructs a black community across time and space as a gift to a world that lacks such community.

Note

1. James W. Coleman, *Blackness and Modernism: The Literary Career of John Edgar Wideman* (Jackson: University Press of Mississippi, 1989). An excerpt from this text is included in part 3 of this volume.

Acknowledgments

Birkerts, Sven. "The Art of Memory." *The New Republic* (13 and 20 July 1992): 42–49. Excerpted by permission of *The New Republic,* ©1992, The New Republic, Inc.

Coleman, James W. *Blackness and Modernism: The Literary Career of John Edgar Wideman.* Jackson: University Press of Mississippi, 1989, 79–80, 81, 95–96. Used by permission of University Press of Mississippi.

Lustig, Jessica. "Home: An Interview with John Edgar Wideman." *African American Review* 26.3 (Fall 1992): 453–56. Used by permission of Jessica Lustig.

Rowell, Charles H. "An Interview with John Edgar Wideman." 13.1 (Winter 1990): 47–60. ©1990. The Johns Hopkins University Press.

Rushdy, Ashraf H.A. "Fraternal Blues: John Edgar Wideman's Homewood Trilogy." *Contemporary Literature* 32.3 (Fall 1991): 312–45. Reprinted by permission of the University of Wisconsin Press.

Samuels, Wilfred D. "Going Home: A Conversation with John Edgar Wideman." *Callaloo* 6.1 (February 1983): 40–59. ©1983. The Johns Hopkins University Press.

Part 1

THE SHORT FICTION

Family History: *Damballah*

Damballah (1981) is a collection of 12 stories that is also part of what has come to be known as the Homewood trilogy. This set, comprising the novels *Hiding Place* (1981) and *Sent for You Yesterday* (1983) in addition to the stories, uses the lives and experiences of a black Pittsburgh neighborhood to express Wideman's vision. Homewood serves in effect as his version of William Faulkner's Yoknapatawpha County in coming to terms with the past and understanding the present. Whereas the novels focus on particular individuals and incidents, the story collection's specific role is to move across generations and to locate within each historical moment a narrative that reveals both distinct individuals and the patterns that make these tales part of a family and community saga.

Damballah opens with a dedication "To Robby," Wideman's brother imprisoned for life. He describes his stories as "letters from home," designed to reclaim the past and connect it with the present. His very choice of the phrase "letters from home" is part of that connection, since, as he reminds his brother, that is the phrase their Aunt Geral used to describe watermelons. This food is a reminder not only of the southern rural past but also of the racial stereotyping that kept Wideman from ever enjoying it. By noting that Robby never shared that fear of labeling and thus could simply eat, the author also points to another purpose for his stories. They are an effort to cross the barriers within a generation that were caused in part by race. By going back to the family narratives, Wideman recovers for himself a relationship to the past and to his racial identity that Robby never lost. Moreover, since the narrator talks in some of the stories about an imprisoned brother, they are efforts to achieve fraternal solidarity, even if the brothers have led very different lives.

This family motif is reinforced by the description of Damballah that follows the dedication. This ancestral spirit is the father figure, the "good serpent" of African and Caribbean religious traditions. He is the symbol of continuity, of the reality of the past, and of the certainty of the future. The design of the collection is implied in a line from the description: "One song invoking Damballah requests that he 'Gather up

3

the family.' "[1] Wideman's stories are precisely such a gathering, thus suggesting that for him the literary serves a spiritual function. The author plays the role of Damballah in telling the experiences of past and present. In effect, he seeks spiritual wholeness by re-creating the family. This process follows an African cultural practice of linking the sacred and the secular, the aesthetic and the functional.

"Damballah"

The first story carries the spirit's name and thereby announces itself as a narrative of origins. It tells of Orion, a slave from Africa who refuses to adapt to his American enslavement. Not only does he reject the English language and Christian faith but he also displays a strong connection with his African background. The story opens with a third-person perspective that allows us to enter Orion's consciousness. We see his oneness with nature, represented as an African trait that reflects not a simplistic black naturalness but a blurring of the boundaries between natural, human, and spiritual worlds: "Orion thought of the eldest priest chalking a design on the floor of the sacred *obi*. Drawing the watery door no living hands could push open, the crossroads where the spirits passed between worlds" (275). He regrets that he did not have the chance to learn the magic words that drew the fish up into the fishermen's baskets. Instead he must rely on his patience and skill to catch the fish with his hands, especially since he refuses to eat any of the food provided by whites.

Because he will not accommodate himself to this "blood-soaked land," the other blacks see him as crazy, and the whites view him as "savage." The only one who pays real attention is the unnamed boy who is the story's central consciousness. The boy follows him to the river and watches as he performs certain rituals. Orion, of course, knows that he is there and wonders if this child can carry on the traditions. He speaks to him the crucial word: "Damballah," in effect giving him the name of the true father and thereby connecting him to the ancestors. But the boy is slapped by his Aunt Lissy when he repeats the word: " 'Don't you ever, you hear me, ever let me hear that heathen talk no more. You hear me, boy? You talk Merican, boy' " (279).

Wideman refuses to sentimentalize the African link; his slaves have adapted themselves to the New World, rejecting the language, religion, and cosmology of the Old. Lissy's statement creates the binary of "heathen" and "Merican" talk, asserting in the process a breaking of history after the Middle Passage of the slave trade. She is the product of a new order, and it is important to forget what went before, to name it the heathen Other. In this way, she can construct for herself and later generations a new identity. But that which is repressed returns and must be denied yet again, this time by slapping the boy.

For the child, it is not repression but knowledge that is desired. Even after the punishment, he returns to Orion, who both enacts rituals and talks about them. He does so in a language unknown to the boy but meaningful nonetheless:

> Orion talked to the emptiness he shaped with his long black fingers. His eyes were closed. Orion wasn't speaking but sounds came from inside him the boy had never heard before, strange words, clicks, whistles and grunts. A singsong moan that rose and fell and floated like the old man's busy hands above the cross. Damballah like a drum beat in the chant. Damballah a place the boy could enter, a familiar sound he began to anticipate, a sound outside of him which slowly forced its way inside, a sound measuring his heartbeat then one with the pumping surge of his blood. (279)

Though what he hears is strange to his American ears, the boy continues to listen, with more than his ears. He begins to enter the sound "Damballah," and then it "forces" its way into him. This interpenetration connects him with the earlier description of Orion's crossing of boundaries.

The cross is Damballah's emblem, standing for the crossroads between spiritual and physical, life and death, nature and man. The boy's "Merican" language is horizontal, moving from subject to verb to object; this language is "crossed" by Orion's "sounds," which move vertically into a spiritual realm. One language orders, names, organizes; the other moves to a higher level. Thus, through his persistence and desire for understanding, the boy stands at the center of a cultural crossroads. He is the true African American. But this is not a moment of choice, of either/or, but rather a sacred space in which he embodies both worlds in all their difference.

It is only appropriate, then, that the boy plays a crucial role at the time of Orion's death. The old man first assaults the overseer and then sits naked on the porch of the plantation house. Beyond their immediate effects, these actions are symbolic revolutionary gestures that signify the overthrow of white authority and expose that authority's exploitation of the black body. For the symbolism as much as the literal acts, Orion is taken to the barn and beheaded, though the execution is not easy. The execution, reported rather than shown, clearly is more disruptive to the whites than appears on the surface. It takes four strong men to carry Orion to the barn, though he offers no resistance. An unidentified scream in the night is the only sound, though when the boy goes into the barn the next morning, he sees evidence of the terror the white men must have felt.

Interrupting the boy's experience is a prayer that on the surface is an appeal for Orion:

> Forgive him, Father. I tried to the end of my patience to restore his lost soul. I made a mighty effort to bring him to the Ark of Salvation but he walked in darkness too long. He mocked Your Grace. He denied Your Word. Have mercy on him and forgive his heathen ways as you forgive the soulless beasts of the fields and birds of the air. (283)

The language is consistent with that of the master's earlier letter to Orion's former owner. Also evident are the master's self-righteousness and arrogance. But the irony is that the same words could be directed against the master. He is the one mocking God by his sexual actions in the slave quarters. He is the one who kills another, thus blasphemously claiming God's prerogatives of mercy and justice for himself. It is also important to note the presence of the other Father, Damballah, whose "word" is denied, whose world is called soulless, and whose priest is attacked. Thus, in the very language of domination, the master is revealed as the moral inferior of the "heathen."

In the closing ritual of the narrative, the boy chooses to embrace his heritage. He takes the severed head of Orion down to the river. There he waits for the ghost to prepare itself. Part of this waiting is his own continuing education. This time he is the one who draws the cross and says the word. But his way of understanding is not Orion's; it is the hybrid of his two worlds: "Damballah said it be a long way a ghost be going and Jordan chilly and wide and a new ghost take his time getting his wings together" (283). The language blends African figures with those of the spirituals. The ghost may be going back home to Africa, but it is doing so on the wings of a Christian angel. The boy becomes the site of the hyphenation African-American, the crossroads of two cultures, two worldviews. He is not the stereotypically servile or tragic mulatto but one who successfully negotiates and lives the differences that make up his heritage.

At the end, he throws the head of Orion into the river, thus beginning the journey home. Like the older man, the boy is described as birdlike, specifically like the crane often represented in West African masking traditions. Also like Orion and the crane, the boy enters the water himself at the end, thus closing the circle of the narrative, which began with Orion doing the same thing. A new sacred space is created, one available now to New World Africans. The legend of Orion becomes the narrative access to the "venerable father."

"Lizabeth: The Caterpillar Story"

"Lizabeth: The Caterpillar Story" is a study of family love in the midst of danger. Each member of the group puts her- or himself at risk in order to save another. This narrative of mutual salvation is told through interlinked stories of the mother Freeda and the daughter Lizabeth. The narrative method also shifts throughout, from dialogue to omniscient voice to limited omniscience, and from the vagaries of memory to objectively told flashback to flash-forward interior monologue. These shifts place in the foreground the process of storytelling as a shaping force in the understanding of the self and the community. Stories are told repeatedly, but the retelling serves only to confirm identity and one's place in the world.

Two fairly simple plotlines underlie the narrative. One involves the title event. When she is a baby, Lizabeth bites the head off a caterpillar. Freeda panics, fearing that her daughter is poisoned. When John French, her husband, comes home, he takes the baby in his arms and then eats the rest of the insect, asserting, "[I]f I don't die, she ain't gonna die neither" (304). This becomes a story often told, especially by Freeda, and is being told on the occasion of the second major event. As Freeda holds the five-year-old Lizabeth in her lap, she watches her husband walk toward the house. Suddenly she screams out a warning and thrusts her hand through the window, thus saving John from being shot in the back.

Within the framework of these two stories is revealed the quality and character of life in the family and in the community. They live in a world of dangers, both natural and man made. As Freeda says of her husband, "It's funny sitting here listening at you talk about your father that way because I never thought about nobody else needing to save him but me. Then I hear you talking and think about John French and know

7

there ain't no way he could have lived long as he did unless a whole lotta people working real hard at saving that crazy man" (301). French is represented throughout *Damballah* as the strongest of the characters, yet that very strength makes him vulnerable and in need of protection. He is proud and assertive, and those qualities make him "crazy" in a black community of the early and mid twentieth century. But he is also a man capable of acts of mundane courage, such as eating the caterpillar.

Woven into the story are other indicators of danger. One day Freeda finds under the icebox a gun that had belonged to Albert Wilkes, a man accused of killing a policeman and whose tale is told in the novel *Sent for You Yesterday* (1983), the third work in the Homewood trilogy. The presence of the gun, even without John French's connection to any crime, puts his family at risk. It potentially gives police the opportunity to implicate yet another black man in crime.

Even as a child Lizabeth understands this reality. When an unknown person begins dumping ashes on the lot he intends as a garden, John French stays up at night with his shotgun, planning to shoot the trespasser. But his daughter knows that if he does so, he will have to run away, just as Albert Wilkes did. That, she fears, would destroy the family. She places herself in a deeply ambiguous position. She stays awake at night listening for the sound of a wheelbarrow. The way to save her father is to betray him; she must warn the intruder of her father's armed presence and thus save all their lives. Since no trespasser appears during this time, Lizabeth is not certain of the effect of her effort. But in her later life, she interprets it as a self-sacrificing, saving act. It is the intensity of the undertaking rather than its outcome that is crucial. It is as though membership in the family is validated through such gestures.

At the same time, it can be argued that the sense of family is constructed through rituals of sacrifice and, more important, through the narratives of these rituals. The stories both express and define the values of this family. Though they have very little, each life is worth everything. There is always something that can be given to support this view. In a world of economic deprivation and racism, purpose and identity are maintained through repetition of the sacrificial narratives. Freeda seeks to keep her family safe in a neighborhood "full of niggers," by which she means inhabited by parents who do not care for their children and do not seek to make better lives for them. She tries to protect her children from that world. Unfortunately for her ambitions, the man she loves is part of that world in his drinking and gambling. Her stories, then, serve both to name that outside reality as dangerous and to reinforce her own alternative vision. The tale of the caterpillar brings John French into that vision by showing his devotion to family.

The story of the ashes, told by Lizabeth, serves a similar function. In it, her father wishes to re-create the kind of garden he had when growing up in Virginia. But the desire to give black Pittsburgh the character of the rural South, and thus to return to a childhood realm of innocence, is only a dream. He has not in fact made any effort to create a garden. The violation of the space through dumping is thus a violation of a dream rather than an act of criminality. The intruder is symbolically all those forces that have kept John French from achieving his desires in life. By holding on to the memory of the episode and her role in it, Lizabeth keeps alive for herself the view of her father as a man with worthy dreams, even if he could not realize them. Telling the story to her mother years after John French's death reaffirms the daughter's place in the world her parents constructed, both in reality and in tales. Freeda reinforces Lizabeth's claim by revising the shooting story so that the daughter's presence prevents the mother from jumping through the window to save her husband. Because Lizabeth sits in her lap, she only cuts her hand. By bringing her into the story as saving agent rather than passive observer, Freeda allows her child to join the parents as one whose saving gesture was unambiguous. Each person thus goes beyond an impulse to save another and has a physical experience that expresses familial devotion. The black body, the symbol so often of subservience, exploitation, and degradation, is made to represent transcendent self-sacrifice.

Story also is used to signify the reality of the self. The narrative offers a flash-forward of Lizabeth:

(Years later when she will have grandchildren of her own and her mother and father both long dead Lizabeth will still be trying to understand why sometimes it takes someone's voice to make things real. She will be sitting in a room and the room full of her children and grandchildren and everybody eating and talking and laughing but she will be staring down a dark tunnel and that dark, empty tunnel is her life, a life in which nothing has happened, and she'll feel like screaming at the darkness and emptiness and wringing her hands because nothing will seem real, and she will be alone in a room full of strangers. She will need to tell someone how it had happened. But anybody who'd care would be long dead. Anybody who'd know what she was talking about would be long gone but she needs to tell someone so she will begin telling herself. Patting her foot on the floor to keep time.

Then she will be speaking out loud. The others will listen and pay attention. She will see down the tunnel and it won't be a tunnel at all, but a door opening on something clear and bright. Something which makes so much sense it will flash sudden and bright as the sky in a summer storm. Telling the story right will make it real. (313–14)

To some extent, this passage reflects Wideman's view of storytelling. The world in his work is frequently represented as a wasteland, without inherent meaning, especially for African Americans. The individual is isolated in contemporary society, which has largely lost the capacity for meaningful communication and understanding. Those who had that capacity are now gone, only ghostly presences that, contrary to African-centered beliefs, can offer nothing in the way of reassurance or nurture. Without a supportive world of either present or past, the self is threatened with disintegration. But that very threat generates voice. In order to be, the self must speak, even if only an interior monologue. It is the nature of human beings to construct an order, about emptiness if necessary. This telling of nothingness paradoxically gives it meaning. Lizabeth finds a rhythm to the emptiness, which gives it shape and thereby makes it communicable. Others can hear the story because, like the blues, it tells the listener's experience by telling that of the speaker.

But this communication takes place only if the story is told "right." It must have the right rhythm, the true detail, the authentic voice. The teller, in other words, must be an artist, capable of shaping the material into the appropriate form. She must take the risk of constructing reality through her narrative skills. Thus Wideman returns to a romantic notion of the artist as interpreter of the world and perhaps even creator of it in the sense of providing meaning. In its narratives, the French family constructs itself, its individual members, its history, and its present. In doing so, its members reflect the most basic human needs and offer what hope is available both in their actions and in the tales of themselves.

"The Songs of Reba Love Jackson"

"The Songs of Reba Love Jackson" turns from stories to songs as the means of communication. On the surface, the narrative concerns the character and experiences of a gospel singer greatly loved in the African-American community. But it also challenges the categories of the sacred and the secular, purity and impurity, appearance and reality. Though

Reba Love herself is presented as consistently good, the idea of goodness itself is scrutinized. One mechanism for this scrutiny is the shifting perspectives of the narrative. We hear the voices of the title character, her mother, an unnamed friend, and Blind Willie, a drunken old blues performer. The story is also broken into short episodes, which often have little in common beyond Reba Love's central role in them. This fragmentation reinforces the dual meaning of the title: we are presented with songs (stories) *by* Reba Love and songs *about* her. Rather than any single episode or voice, the combination of many of each provides the fullest version of her; the reader must make the connections. In that sense, the reader composes her own song.

An appropriate place to begin this composition is Reba Love's celebrity image, represented through a radio interview that occurs in the middle of the story. Crucial to this episode is the conflict between the announcer's projection of her as a conventional star and her competing self-representation. The announcer opens by emphasizing the event rather than the person. For him, the interview is simply part of a promotional effort; he barely mentions her name in his introduction. When she describes her birth and early childhood in the South, he interrupts to emphasize the regional stereotype:

> Yes siree. Down home country. We knows all about it, don't we? Fried chicken and biscuits and grits and the preacher coming over on Sunday wolfing down half the platter . . . Lawd . . . Lawd . . . Lawd. (362)

His parody of southern speech and of the church could easily be taken as an affront to her, but he is more interested in entertaining his audience.

He then invites a comment about her political views, of which she claims to have none. She sees her advocacy of rights as simply an extension of the message of her songs, which emphasize dignity, morality, and divine rather than human obedience. What is clearly for her the main point is for him a potentially embarrassing digression. He tries to turn the discussion to her rise to stardom, but she keeps going back to the awkward and often humiliating moments of life in a racist society. She is willing to narrate her calling, but he insists on a tale of the rise to fame.

Finally he cuts her off and substitutes an old review of a performance in France for her self-portrait: " 'Reba Love Jackson galvanizes the audience. . . . No lady on the stage but a roaring black pantheress, leaping,

11

bounding, dancing her songs . . . , she embodies what is primitive and powerful in the African soul' " (365). She seeks to displace this racist discourse with her own more spiritual interpretation of her performance. The announcer, however, prefers the reading of "the French soul brother." He disregards the dehumanizing and insulting character of the comment in his desire to produce an enticing packaging of Reba Love.

The episode serves as a critique of the effects of media on storytelling and self-definition. Her story is emptied of its real significance in order to fit a preestablished image of the black woman. Her blackness is a series of clichés, not a life story. One irony operating here is the need of black media to use the same discursive practices as those of whites. To call the French journalist a "soul brother" while reducing Reba Love to animal status suggests the extent to which mass culture transcends both national and racial boundaries. The commodification of the gospel singer indicates that the two men have the same capitalist soul, one uninterested in spiritual or political reality.

This episode is the most pronounced in its emphasis on the tension between projections of Reba Love and her self-understanding. A more complex example concerns her mother, Precious Pearl. The story opens with the daughter's dedication of her music to the memory of her mother, "the one who loved me best on this earth" (352). But this same mother lived a life of frustration and bitterness. She despised the drunken husband who abandoned her and her daughter, and every man who reminded her of him. She hated the world in which they had to live. Wideman portrays her as somewhat mad:

> She wondered how it would feel to fly closer to the sun. To have it burn the tacky clothes from her back, and then the skin gone too, all the flesh dropping away like old clothes till the soul rises naked to the Father's side. Precious Jackson looks down at the gray pavement. She is tall and black and rail thin. Her cropped hair is plastered to her skull by a black net cap. Her round, pop eyes are full and hungry; they burn like the eyes of the saints who never sleep. (355)

This desire for purity is a rejection of the life of the community in all its ordinary, fallible humanness; it is also a profound fear of that world. Precious wishes God's punishment on the drunken man in the street, in part because he has a beautiful voice that can perform both hymns and blues. It is not surprising that the daughter who finds her spirituality in embracing rather than rejecting the world violates many of her mother's rules. She has sex at age 13 and worries not about the morality but about the patched underwear that the boy might see. Later she acknowledges the importance of the drunk, calling him the one "who taught me to sing" (354).

Reba Love attempts to accept everything but worries sometimes that her self will be lost in the process: "Is there ever any other way she asked herself? Am I to be Reba Love Jackson all the days of my life?" (361). "Reba Love Jackson" is less a person than a projection of all the needs of ordinary people and a promise of satisfaction. The stories that are her songs narrate those desires and tell the needy that they are not alone. Her claim of ordinariness validates her for her audiences; she sings their experience and proclaims that it can be lived through, in part by attention to the songs. She orders their troubles and desires as they cannot and thus gives meaning to their lives.

But the need for her to go on being Reba Love Jackson also indicates the unending suffering in the world. Her faith and her music do not change that reality. Blind Willie gets thrown out of bars for singing "nasty blues." The world of Homewood has not changed for the better since her mother dreaded walking its streets. And death keeps taking more people, leaving the living to mourn. The songs are a moment of relief, not a solution. Whatever Reba Love believes, her creator persists in a hopeless but necessary belief in the power of the artist's voice.

"Across the Wide Missouri"

A parallel to the story of mother and daughter is that of father and son in "Across the Wide Missouri." If "Damballah" is a story of the quest for the ancestral father, "Across" narrates the search for the all-too-real biological father. More precisely, it is an attempt to define the father-son relationship. This is a theme to which Wideman will return in *Fatheralong* (1994), which he subtitles *A Meditation on Fathers and Sons, Race and Society*. As that subtitle suggests, he always finds that the personal relationship is caught up in social issues. The father is never simply an individual but is always also a symbol of the possibilities and limitations of being black and male in American society. In this sense, the references to John French that run through the stories provide a standard for assessing and understanding black masculinity across generations.

This theme also invites a psychocultural reading, if not necessarily a psychoanalytical one. If the father conventionally represents a figure of authority and thus both threat and model for the son, then the position of the black father in a racist society is highly problematic. Such a man lacks economic, political, and social power and thus can be seen as impotent by his son; moreover, if, as Jacques Lacan argues, the father symbolizes the law,[2] then the black man, stereotyped as criminal, can never embody legitimate authority. The real power, the true father, in this sense must always be the white man.

"Across the Wide Missouri" opens precisely in such ambiguity. The first-person narrator begins in confusion because he keeps remembering Clark Gable in a movie when he thinks about his father. Gable's character has élan, sophistication, and a sense of control over his world. In a telling comment, the narrator says, "The white man in the mirror [a scene from the movie] is my father" (371). In contrast, the real father is a waiter in a department store dining room, dependent on an appearance at least of cheerful subservience to whites for his income. What brings the narrator back from his confused memory is the recollection of his mother telling him about a childhood visit to his father's workplace. But even this memory is faulty, since the "facts" of the incident include being accompanied by his mother to the store. In fact, the story is as much about how the past is constructed, especially as narrative, as it is about the events themselves. The narrator repeatedly notes that he has told about this experience before but that this time he wants to get it right. The new version includes details left out before, perhaps because of their emotional weight:

> So my mother pointed to the large, red-carpeted room and I remember wanting to kiss her, to wait with her at the elevators after she pushed the button and the green arrow pointed down. If I had written it that way the first time I would be kissing her again and smelling her perfume and hearing the bells and steel pulleys of the elevators and staring again apprehensively through the back of my head at the cavernous room full of white people and the black men in white coats moving silently as ghosts but none of them my father. (371–72)

The reason for excluding this moment in previous versions (none of which readers see) and for framing it in this one is to create a distance from the mother in order to seek the father. The mother is emotional support and sustenance, a space of security and warmth. The earlier story apparently follows the narrative convention of the young man going forth alone to encounter a male world. The nature of that world is indicated by what the boy sees "through the back of [his] head": the alien and threatening space of the father. To enter that "cavernous" world, the child must literally turn his back on the mother and risk the loss of her protection and guidance. Thus the revision of his narrative reveals the self as much more vulnerable and insecure than the conventional story would allow.

This condition is reinforced by the initial absence of the father from "his" space, leaving the son confused about his behavior and prospects. He is silenced and intimidated by the "white" territory he must enter. He experiences shame in the situation, owing partly to a sense that he has no right to enter this realm. This sensation is associated with two incidents from different periods in the narrator's life. The first is a flash-forward:

> Outside the judge's chambers in the marble halls of the courthouse, years later waiting to plead for my brother, I felt the same intimidation, the same need to remind myself that I had a right to be where I was. That the message coded into the walls and doors and ceilings and floors, into the substances of which they were made, could be confronted, that I could talk and breathe in the storm of words flung at me by the invisible architects who had disciplined the space in which I found myself. (372)

The flashback is associated with a more intimate moment. The boy stands outside his father's room as the older man sleeps. He calls to him even though he has been warned that his father had worked late and needs to sleep. He soaks in the aura of paternity:

> [B]ut I am there, on the cold linoleum listening to him snore, smelling his sleep, the man smell I wonder now if I've inherited so it trails me, and stamps my things mine when my kids are messing around where they shouldn't be. I am talking to myself when he stirs in that darkness behind the curtain. He groans and the mattress groans under him and the green metal cot squeaks as he shifts to another place in his dreaming. (372–73)

These three moments have in common the position of the son as outsider, doubtful of his right to be where he is. The flash-forward returns us to his relationship to the law. He must claim a voice and a place in a space that he perceives denies them to him. The building itself carries "messages" of his exclusion as he stands outside the inner sanctum of the white father figure, who is also the embodiment of the law. He is there on the side of his guilty brother and thus is himself associated with criminality. Crucial to his self-image is the extent to which he accepts this definition of his being, even in his adulthood. He must fight not what is directly asserted but what he himself reads into his situation.

The other scene, although it places the son on the margin, does the same with the father. His room is itself liminal space, located on a landing outside the apartment; his "green metal cot" indicates his isolation from a patriarchal position of social and sexual power. The son is in fact more "inside" than the father in this black household. The man that the son tries to make the center of his narrative is marginalized in the most intimate of spaces. The source of his placement is not specified in the story. He is an absent presence, one whose status is everywhere ambiguous. The "smell" that identifies him must be in part one of impotence.

In the restaurant, not only is he for the moment not visible, but the black waiters are themselves not quite real:

> I stare at all the black faces. They won't stay still. Bobbing and bowing into the white faces or gliding toward the far swinging doors, the closely cropped heads poised and impenetrable above mandarin collars. Toomer called the white faces petals of dusk and I think now of the waiters insinuating themselves like birds into clusters of petals, dipping silently, silently depositing pollen or whatever makes flowers grow and white people be nice to black people.... Dark faces never still long enough to be my father. (373)

The black men are too much alike in their fluttering yet "impenetrable" role of subservience to be individually distinguishable. They are in fact nothing other than the role they play, a role that the narrator naturalizes by his metaphor of pollination. At the same time, he problematizes that notion through the allusions to Chinese culture. "Impenetrable" echoes "inscrutable," an Orientalist label for that "alien" society, and "mandarin" suggests the sophistication and difficulty of that culture. The mixing of metaphors here enhances the unreality of the scene and the ambiguous status of the waiters. Whether they are controlled or controlling is unclear. Since one of them (the son cannot tell which) is the father, the uncertainty reinforces the complexity of the father-son relationship.

The child, by contrast, knows that he is an interloper with no defined role. He is overwhelmed by the whiteness that is the dining room. When he discovers change under the saucers of the uncleared table at which he is seated, he is certain that whites will return and accuse him of theft. He creates a scenario in which he is a small being fouling the whiteness by his very presence and bound to be condemned by white authority of lying and theft. He deals with the situation by acting out the role he has assigned to himself; he takes the coins and then wishes himself invisible. Having no experience of tipping, he believes that he is stealing from whites, not from the waiters. He has already learned an ultimately self-destructive lesson: if the world already assumes guilt, he might as well get what he can out of the situation.

When the father arrives, the talk between them, unlike that between the waiters, is sparse and awkward. Again the narrator points out that this is a revision of the earlier story, in which he included "[a] lot of conversation broken by stage directions and the intrusions of restaurant business and restaurant noise" (374). The point of the revision seems to be, first, to reflect more accurately the dynamics of the family, and second, to refute any negative reading of this pattern. The two of them have always been "constrained" in talk, but the narrator points out that it is the father's presence, not his words, that matters. "Point was he was with me and would stay with me the whole afternoon" (374). The father becomes godlike in the recollection, a figure whose being alone is sufficiently worthy of devotion. Thus his distance and marginality are replaced in the memory with his authority and his beauty. The narrator also recalls a set of amusement-park photographs of his parents. In them, his father appears much darker than he actually is. But what the son recalls is that he appears handsome and self-possessed, qualities that remain despite his circumstances.

These details are important because the movie they see that afternoon is *Across the Wide Missouri*, starring Clark Gable. Rather than discussing the movie, the narrator focuses on the song, which he insists he remembers only in fragments. The forgetting seems deliberate: "I think I don't know the words on purpose" (376). The reason for this lapse is emotional; he feels like crying each time he hears all or part of the song. The reason for the emotion is left vague, but it is connected to his relationships with his father and his own son. The son learned the song, which he called "Shenandoah," for a school program, a program the narrator failed to attend because he preferred to entertain a visiting poet. The father, of course, is associated with the movie and with the opening of the story, in which Gable becomes the father: "Like taking me to the movies once, alone, just the two of us in a downtown theater and seeing him for the whole ninety minutes doing good and being brave and handsome and thundering like a god across the screen. Or brushing his teeth loudly in the morning at the sink" (377).

The language here revises the opening passage. The narrator does not wish the father to be a powerful white man; the movie star is in fact a version of the father, carrying his authority and dignity wherever he is and whatever he is doing. The sorrow of the passage is neither frustrated desire for some alternative family history nor sadness at the father's marginality. Rather, it is recognition of the limited opportunities for father-son interaction. The circumstances of the father's life allowed few moments like the afternoon at the movie, and the narrator now understands what was lost.

As a father himself, he also appreciates what it means to have sons, and thus he feels a little of what his father must have experienced as a parent. The situations of fatherhood are different; the narrator has time and money to spend on and with his sons. But this changes neither the father's desire to be heroic nor the child's anxiety. He says of his child, the one who carries the father's name as a middle name:

> But he forgets lots of things. He's the kind of kid who forgets lots of things but who remembers everything. He has the gift of feeling. Things don't touch him, they imprint. You can see it sometimes. And it hurts. He already knows he will suffer for whatever he knows. Maybe that's why he forgets so much. (378)

In this closing passage, the narrator is clearly describing the self of the story as well as his son. He may also be describing the father, who seems very much aware of the complexities of his own life. The forgetting is necessary not because life is traumatic, though it is sometimes that, but because there are limits that simply cannot be overcome. The sons desire the father's presence and wish him to be godlike and are frustrated that these desires cannot be satisfied. The fathers, desiring authority and power, find themselves experiencing guilt and impotence because of individual and social limitations. Given life's other unavoidable struggles, this most personal one seems especially painful. Forgetting is better. But of course, as the story demonstrates, there is no true forgetting. There is instead evasion and repression. The existence of an earlier version of the story suggests the narrator's effort to construct a happy tale, a tale he knows is false.

But it can be argued that the new version should also not be trusted. It offers its own happy ending. We have the identity of generations and the narrator's achievement of insight, sympathy, and resolution. He knows what his father experienced and what his son will experience, and he has come to terms with his own conflicts. Although he cannot prevent his son's "suffering," his awareness allows for preparation and amelioration. But the story still suppresses and evades. Refusing to come to terms with the father's position in his own household means that some aspect of his personality and family dynamic has not been explored. If we are to take the narrative as psychologically significant, then the father-mother relationship is crucial both to the son and to the story. Is this decentered status one of the qualities admired or one that must be overlooked? Similarly, the father is both among and absent from the ghostly waiters in the restaurant. He has, at best, ambiguous control and power in the workplace. Such facts suggest his difference from, not similarity to, Clark Gable in the movie. Identification in this case is imposed, not achieved. Moreover, the narrator, in his role as father, does not seem to have benefited from his own experience. He does not indicate a close relationship with his sons, though he spends more time with them than his father did with him. He neglects them, as in the case of the music program, without sensing how they might respond. He is strangely distant from the son who will suffer, presenting the information more as objective observation than as parental concern.

The implication of such a reading is that Wideman is truly postmodern in his perspective. Contrary to the title of his third collection, perhaps no stories are true, in the sense that they inevitably build in discontinuities and distortions. Their "authenticity" is not in accurately reflecting a real or fictional world but in their representation of the struggle to speak what is ultimately unspeakable.

"Tommy"

"Tommy" is a study of a world without fathers and thus without any meaningful authority. It is the story of the wasteland that Homewood has become by the 1970s. It is also a version of the story of Robby, Wideman's brother, a story more fully developed in *Brothers and Keepers* (1984). Robby, to whom *Damballah* is dedicated, is serving a life-without-parole prison sentence for his participation in a robbery in which a killing occurred. In "Tommy," Wideman describes the harsh environment in which inmates live and then narrates the crime itself. A refrain running through the tale is "Nothing to it," a street expression that suggests that everything is easy but that in context also connotes existential despair. There is "nothing" to Homewood, to Tommy's life or the lives of his companions, to the future. In such circumstances criminal acts to get money are easy to conceive—there is "nothing to it."

The first half of the story is structured as a journey through the contemporary wasteland. Seen through Tommy's consciousness, Homewood is a place of ruin, decay, and silence. Unlike classical quests or pilgrimages, the protagonist here has no guide or high moral purpose. Unlike other narratives in *Damballah*, this one offers no hope or meaning. It opens with Tommy looking for his uncle Carl, who would be willing to buy him a drink. When he cannot be found in the Velvet Slipper, where Tommy finds "just the jukebox and beer smell and the stink from the men's room door always hanging open" (389), he knows that his uncle is at the clinic getting his methadone. Within this first paragraph, we see the failure of the male elders to provide any direction for younger men. They have their own troubles and dependencies and so cannot be a resource for others. The heroic ancestors and somewhat marginalized fathers of earlier stories become the embodiment of failure here. In place of the voices of the past, there is only "nigger music and nigger talk" (389), terms used in a highly derogatory manner.

Outside, what had been the center of Homewood is nothing but abandoned buildings, empty lots, and broken parking meters. They are measures of the loss of vitality and neighborhood. But the past was not golden or even particularly pleasant. Consistently, the memories evoked by places are highly ambivalent. Tommy recalls that as a child, he made money by carrying groceries for neighborhood women. The boys vied for white customers, because they tipped generously. The black women, who were matrons of the church, made them work much harder for far less money. In addition, youthful sexual exploits are associated with missing the last trolley and thus a long walk.

The present is so hopeless that Tommy has a momentary apocalyptic vision:

> Somebody should make a deep ditch out of Homewood Avenue and just go on and push the row houses and boarded storefronts into the hole. Bury it all, like in a movie he had seen a dam burst and the flood waters ripping through the dry bed of a river till the roaring water overflowed the banks and swept away trees and houses, uprooting everything in its path like a cleansing wind. (390)

The thought piles on rather than develops the imagery. Burial, flood, and wind are brought together in the effort to represent the obliteration of Homewood. None of the figures seems sufficient by itself: burial leaves traces, and floods leave residue. Only in combination with the "cleansing" wind are these adequate to the task of complete annihilation. Tommy wishes for the place not to be, in part because the ruins not only symbolize present frustration but also measure the steep decline from even an imperfect past. Only by wiping it all out can anything new be started. Behind one boarded-up storefront are remnants of posters: "Self-defense demonstration . . . Ahmed Jamal. Rummage Sale. Omega Boat Ride. The Dells. Madame Walker's Beauty Products" (393). These signify a lost community, with its militance, entertainment, community activities, and standards. There is no longer a community to defend, valuable items to sell, music to provide, or beauty to maintain. The memories are burdens, one source of the bitterness and hostility that pervades the streets. They are reminders of failure, defeat, and exploitation.

Like the places, the people are ruins. Anonymous voices in the pool halls try to borrow a quarter, with an insincere promise to pay it right back. Young men have no respect for or fear of anything and will kill even the elders for a little money. "Niggers write all over everything don't even know how to spell. Drawing power fists that look like a loaf of bread" (392). People park in the middle of the street and ignore those trying to get by. The text itself reflects the lack of consideration for the people; all are incompetent, self-centered, aimless, and verbally if not physically violent. Even the basketball players, elsewhere in Wideman's writing an emblem of energy and creativity, are said to exert themselves more for the games than they ever did for work. Tommy brings together place and people in another of his conceits:

> Thinking this whole Avenue is like somebody's mouth they let some jive dentist fuck with. All these old houses nothing but rotten teeth and these raggedy pits is where some been dug out or knocked out and ain't nothing left but stumps and snaggleteeth just waiting to go. Thinking, that's right. That's just what it is. Why it stinks around here and why ain't nothing but filth and germs and rot. And what that make me? What it make all these niggers? Thinking yes, yes, that's all it is. (392)

Violence, neglect, and corruption have created a condition not merely of decay but of irreparable rot. The blame for this is diffuse: after all, the "somebody" allowed the "jive dentist" to do his work. And the people are part of the rot. Self-hatred has become central to their identity and to Tommy's. His use of the word *nigger* in this context indicates a return to a derogatory, insulting connotation in contrast to the efforts in (primarily) male African-American communities to redefine the word as an affirmative, affiliative term. In Tommy's usage, it comes close to its original white racist meaning.

The second half of the story narrates the criminal action that devolves from these conditions and perspectives. Much of this section is straightforward narration, unlike the interior monologue of the first half. The early aimless wandering and thinking becomes destructively focused action. Tommy locates his friends, including Ruchell, and sees that they are high on drugs, even though it is early in the day. Ruchell explains that the scam he is planning will work because of the greed and racism of the white man involved. Indovina assumes that blacks are too stupid to outsmart him. Like tricksters of folk tradition, they count on being able to manipulate his arrogance to their advantage.

This story line is interrupted as Tommy offers his brother John an explanation:

> "When you ain't got nothing you get desperate. You don't care. I mean what you got to be worried about? Your life ain't shit. All you got is a high. Getting high and spending all your time hustling some money so you can get high again. You do anything. Nothing don't matter. . . . A man needs something. A little money in his pocket. I mean you see people around you and on TV and shit. Man, they got everything. Cars and clothes. They can do something for a woman. They got something and you look at yourself in the mirror you're going nowhere. Not a penny in your pocket. Your own people disgusted with you. Begging around your family like a little kid or something. And jail and stealing money from your own mama. You get desperate. You do what you have to do." (401)

The passage suggests an inability to function according to the terms of contemporary culture. Drugs serve as an escape from the self-hatred described earlier. Tommy and those like him have been left behind and can do nothing in the legitimate world to catch up. But the drugs are themselves a commodity within consumer culture and thus require money. Thus he is entrapped in an economic order, even if at the bottom. Making money remains essential. But the means of doing so in his world are either criminal or humiliating, thus reinforcing alienation. To have worth and to be valued require having things; even intimate relationships are tied to materiality: "They can do something for a woman." Because manhood and identity are linked to money, even in a place where there is very little of it, the greater the need to demonstrate those qualities, the greater the desperation for money. By Tommy's analysis, the robbery Ruchell plans is a natural consequence of the world of Homewood.

The intrusion of this monologue is necessitated by Wideman's commitment to the voices of the community, including those of the dispossessed and criminal. But it is a voice different from Tommy's street voice; it is closer to that of his educated brother. It is precise in its personal and cultural analysis, suggesting a desire to humanize those who have been dehumanized through the narrative. At the very moment Tommy engages in his most desperate act, his voice is thoughtful and socially aware. In the voice and the self it represents, Wideman problematizes the reader's impulse to reject Tommy as the human refuse he has been describing.

The robbery itself fails because Ruchell does not know how to respond to Chubby, the black employee willing to fight to protect the white man's interest. Panic-stricken, Ruchell kills him, and the thieves flee without getting any of the money. In effect, they validate the view of them as incompetent. They can do nothing but run, having known all along that they are powerless against the justice system.

They end up at John's home in the West on their way to Los Angeles. It is Christmas Eve. While Tommy and John discuss the situation, Ruchell plays army and cowboys and Indians with the children. He in effect returns to the childhood state that Tommy described as so humiliating. After all the despair and frustration of the story, it ends by suggesting that hope itself may be implicated in the despair. He thinks of the children:

> Christmas morning and they never really went to sleep. Looking out the black windows all night for reindeer and shit. Cheating. Worried that all the gifts will turn to ashes if they get caught cheating, but needing to know, to see if reindeer really can fly. (406)

It is in fact the need to believe in something, in the possibility of transcendent magic, that motivates the Ruchells of the world as much as the children. Lacking power, voice, and status, the young men of Homewood seek the "magic" of drugs and criminal activity. The robbery itself was designed, according to Tommy, to finance a new start in a new place. Since nothing can be done through one's own efforts, because in the eyes of the nation, the community, and himself, he is worth nothing, the only possibility is outside the self, in the products of illusion and desperation. The only alternative to such misguided hope is death.

"Solitary"

"Solitary" is a companion piece to "Tommy," as its title might suggest. It takes the perspective of Tommy's mother, Lizabeth, after he is imprisoned. She too walks the streets of Homewood and sees many of the things he had seen. The difference is that her experience comes after she visits him in prison. This context gives her, if anything, a more despairing view of the community.

The story opens with her description of the journey to the prison, which she calls "the other world." The trip, which often takes many hours, involves several changes of buses and, frequently, long waits. It seems to her designed specifically as a punishment for the families of the inmates. In that universe, she loses her identity and dignity, much as the prisoners do:

> The trips were supposed to speak to her plainly. Somebody had arranged it that way. An evil somebody who didn't miss a trick. They said to reach him you must suffer, you must fight the heat and cold, you must sit alone and be beaten by your thoughts, you must forget who you are and be prepared to surrender your dignity just as you surrender your purse to the guard caged outside the waiting room entrance. In the prison world, the world you must die a little to enter, the man you've traveled so far to see is not your son but a number. (408)

The visitor in effect becomes one with the prison; the only way to be in that world is to become part of it. To do so requires losing everything you are: "To enter you must be prepared to leave everything behind and be prepared when you begin the journey home to lose everything again" (408). What Wideman suggests here is a brutal system that dehumanizes everything that engages it. In these observations, he strips away all the reader's assumptions about the function and character of prison life. It is not so much a human institution as a self-governing mechanism having little to do with justice or rehabilitation. Its treatment of families indicates its all-consuming, destructive character.

The return home is in some ways even more disruptive to the mother's self. Not only must she try to recover from the insult to her selfhood, but she also must come to terms with what her son is becoming through this experience. At the same time, she must construct a persona that can engage those who will want to know about him. She must pretend an optimism she does not feel. Moreover, leaving means that she must begin preparing her mind for the next visit:

> She knows what it costs her: the sleepless nights, the rage and helplessness, the utter trembling exhaustion bracketing the journey. How she must fight back tears when she sees his face, hears his voice. How guilt and anger alternate as she avoids people's faces and shrinks into a corner of a bus. She prays the strangers won't see her secrets, won't laugh at her shame, won't shatter in the icy waves of hatred pouring from her frozen heart. She knows her blood pressure will soar sky high and the spasms of dizziness, of nausea will nearly knock her off her feet. (409)

She must endure this physical, psychological, and emotional trauma in order to spend a short time with a son who spends the period they have together berating her for his pain. He accuses her variously of taking too much or too little care of him, of loving too much or too little. She understands that such attacks are his way of coming to terms with who he is and what he has done. But she experiences pain and anger nonetheless: "Did he think he had a right to take out his frustrations on her just because she was the only one who'd listen, who'd travel the million miles to where he was caged?" (411).

The situation described thus far makes "Solitary" consistent with "Tommy." The frustration and despair have simply been shifted to a different generation. The title expands the troubles from the imprisoned to the one whose isolation is not diminished by her "freedom." But the story has a larger significance because the mother's solitude includes a threat to her religious faith and a sense of the loss of family. In contrast to her son, who seems to have had little connection with either faith or family, she has defined her very being by these two elements. As a measure of the difference in perspectives, the mother has a moment of apocalyptic desire parallel to her son's: "Surely the walls [of the prison] weren't too tall, too thick for Him. He could come as a cloud, as a cleansing wind" (409). Tommy's imagery of the wind is drawn from the movies; Lizabeth's, from the Bible. Despite this vision, she is not certain that

God can reach into the prison: "Sometimes she says that to herself, says the prison is a place her God has forsaken. But if He is not there, if His Grace does not touch her son then she too is dwelling in the shadow of unlove" (409). The apparent silence of God, the unremitting suffering that she and her son must endure, suggest a world truly bereft of hope.

In order to move beyond that despair, she must go through rather than evade it. She consciously refuses the succor she might find in her church:

> She knew that she'd find silence there and knew at the foot of the purple-carpeted aisle she could drop to her knees in a familiar place and her God would listen. That if she left her pride in the ravaged street and abandoned her hate and put off her questions He would take her to His bosom. He would bathe her in the fount of His Grace and under-stand and say well done.... She believed that and believed that the plan would reveal His goodness but this long day she could only sees gaps and holes, the way things didn't connect or make sense. (414)

On this particular day, the need is not to escape the pain and anger, because to do so, she sees, would only perpetuate it. Within the space of the church, she can find comfort but not answers. To "abandon" her hate and "put off" her questions would only defer the problems they imply. The God within the church cannot bring resolution, and that is what she now needs. In effect, she wants the pride and hate recognized as legitimate, as valid responses to the situation of her and her son.

To achieve this recognition, she must turn on this day from the church to her other resource, the family. What she expects to find there is something similar to the comfort of God. Instead, following the path of memory, she finds "gaps and holes" there also. Her walk through the neighborhood, unlike the otherwise similar one her son takes in "Tommy," takes her through not only a wasteland but a valley of recollection. Down Homewood Avenue, where the buildings are now burned or abandoned, she recalls John French "strutting like he owned Homewood" (413). By walking the street she can be accompanied by the memories of "her father, her sons, the man she married." She can conjure up the family and community that once was here; unlike Tommy, she finds the past a source of comfort.

But to get through her troubles, she must go deeper into memory and into the neighborhood. She must go to the park where Tommy found his friends and began his catastrophe. But her reason for going there is profoundly different; it is not his life she needs to understand but her own. The journey to the park takes her even further into family history. She passes the monument to World War I veterans that includes her relatives. She passes the place where she went to school and where her great-great-grandfather Charley Bell founded Homewood. The walk reminds her of the changes that have taken place: the loss of racial mix and the resultant neglect by an indifferent city government. It also takes her by the stop on the railroad created for George Westinghouse, who "owned half of Pittsburgh." The stop is now gutted, another reminder of the fleeting nature of power.

Lizabeth finds herself unable to cross the footbridge that leads into Westinghouse Park. She can see into the park and is reminded of the regular visits there in her childhood. Significantly, Wideman does not tell us at this point why she cannot enter the park, only that she can recall her mother's comments about her own and other children running and playing. Rather than explaining, the author breaks the scene to take Lizabeth to the bar where her brother Carl spends his afternoons. This is the same bar where Tommy looked for him. What the young man noted as the old man's frail walk, the woman sees as the slow, confident gait inherited from their father. Moreover, whereas Tommy sought a free drink from his uncle, Lizabeth seeks emotional support from her brother. She wants him to walk with her to the park. Carl is the one she does not have to deceive about her inner struggle; he has been there all along. He expresses concern, but he does not minimize or evade the difficulty. With him, she can get to the heart of the matter:

> "It's God I'm losing. It's Him in me that's slipping away. It happened in the middle of the bridge. I was looking down and looking over into the park. I was thinking about all those times I'd been to Westinghouse Park before. So much on my mind it wasn't really like thinking. More like being on fire all over your body and rushing around trying to beat down the flames in a hundred places at once and doing nothing but making it worse. Then I couldn't take another step. I saw Mama the way she got after her stroke, the way she stopped talking and walking after Daddy died. You remember the evil look she turned on anybody when they mentioned church or praying. . . . I knew why she cursed Him and put God out of her life when she started talking again. I knew if I took another step I'd be like her." (418)

Significantly, what Carl offers is not reassurance about God but belief in the family. What worries Lizabeth in this moment of insight is that she will be alone without God, but her brother insists that the family never leaves anyone alone. Although her faith is so deeply ingrained and of such long standing that her brother's words do not quite make sense, something at that moment gives her strength. Suddenly, God is reconceived not as mercy but as threat and challenge. As a train comes down the track under the footbridge, she recalls her old fear: "She wouldn't know whether to run across or leap under the churning wheels" (419). God becomes the train and thus the terror: "The black bullet would slam into her. Would tear her apart. He could strike you dead in the twinkling of an eye. He killed with thunder and lightning" (419).

But in part because of her brother's presence and his words (though she does not say so), she is willing to confront such a God:

> She stopped again. Made Carl stop with her in the middle of the bridge, at the place she had halted before. She'd wait this time, hold her ground this time. She'd watch it grow larger and larger and not look away, not shut her ears or stop her heart. She'd wait there on the shuddering bridge and see. (419)

In these final words of the story, she chooses to face her fear, doubt, and frustration rather than seek release or comfort. She refuses to sacrifice herself any longer for God or her son. In the presence of the family, represented by Carl, she is willing and able to endure whatever comes. The meaning of family and memory is not nostalgia or escape but courage in the face of overwhelming circumstances. Her faith in herself is the true test, not her belief in God or the past or the future, because it is only that most personal faith that makes the others meaningful.

"Solitary" offers an alternative to the fatalism and illusion of "Tommy." Lizabeth, unlike her son, retains connections with the past, including the church. She sees none of it as a source of self-hatred or exploitation. But Wideman's point is not an essentially conservative one, that holding on to traditions necessarily makes the world a better place or the person a happier one. Rather, his contention is more tough minded: memory and family (and the church) can provide resources to engage a world that is hostile and perhaps even doomed. They make it possible not necessarily to change the world but to have the courage to face the worst that it can offer. Tommy will not be freed by his mother's self-affirmation, nor will the pain of her repeated journeys be lessened. Instead, she will be able to endure the journeys, even if God is silent, and perhaps to pass something of her strength on to her son.

"The Beginnings of Homewood"

The final story of *Damballah* takes readers back to the beginning of the collection as well as to the origin of the family. The narrator opens the story by declaring it defective, because it implicitly contains a letter that he never sent to his imprisoned brother. The first paragraph is in fact an apology to the brother for this failure: "I began by trying to say some things to you, but they never got sent, never reached you so there is something wrong about the story nothing can fix" (420). This notion returns the reader to the dedication of the book to Robby, to whom the stories are addressed as letters. A crucial question is the sense in which these pieces operate as letters for that select audience. Certainly given the tone of "Tommy" and "Across the Wide Missouri," as well as others, they are not epistles of optimism or encouragement; even the more affirmative pieces offer little in the way of hope. The complex message of "The Beginnings of Homewood," with its emphasis again on voices, family, and responsibility, suggests the underlying meaning of these "letters."

The opening paragraph serves to make the narrator complicit in responsibility and guilt within the family. His failure to communicate with his brother implies the value and necessity of voices in keeping alive connections, with both the past and the present. The story the narrator wished to tell his brother was in fact supposed to be a simple one: a slave narrative with its dash to freedom and its happy-ever-after life in the North. It is in many ways a conventional story, but a useful one in that it belongs to their family. Its message would have seemed clear to Tommy/Robby: within their family is an example of overcoming imprisonment, in this case taking the form of slavery, so there is always hope. "What was not simple was the crime of this female runaway set against your crime. What was not simple was my need to tell Sybela's story so it connected with yours" (422). The reason this is not simple is, first, that Sybela's "crime" is only one within a system of oppression and inhumanity, whereas Tommy's is one that, no matter how sympathetic one might be, cannot be read as a moral act. Second, the narrator as story-teller must make the link between experiences widely separated by time and circumstances so that he does not deprive either one of its full significance.

Previous stories have indicated the complexity of Tommy's experience; this one opens up rather than simplifies the meaning of Sybela's. The layers of her tale begin with her name. The narrator speculates that it was a version of Sybil, the priestess denied her voice by being changed into a bird. Thus the name fits the fate of a black female slave denied control over her being. In addition, the slaves referred to her as Belle, in part to counteract masters' practice of giving slaves names that were designed to be parodies of their condition. But the name Belle also referred to an African woman who once lived on the plantation and who had been punished for refusing the sexual advances of the master by having a cage fastened to her head with a bell attached.

> [N]aturally they had started calling her Bell, in derision at first, mock-ing her pride, her futile stubbornness on a point most of the women had conceded long before, a point which peopled the plantation with babies as varied in hue as the many colors of Joseph's coat, then Belle because she had not broken, Mother Belle finally because she was mar-tyr and saint, walking among them with the horrible contraption on her shoulders but unwavering, straight and tall as the day the iron cage had been fitted to her. (423)

The younger Belle is said to resemble this older one, "a reincarnation almost of the queenly, untouchable one who had been sent to suffer with them" (423).

In Mother Belle we have the female equivalent of Orion, the African who refuses to be an accomplice in her reification. Whatever is done to her is a comment on her assailants, not on her. Her great refusal may be "futile" in some practical sense, but it does represent an alternative to the dehumanization of blacks attempted by masters. It gives slaves, including those weaker than she, a different model and ideal than that imposed by the dominant order.

If Sybela were simply the reincarnation of Mother Belle, then the story would have some value as myth, but in fact she is not. She has two children by the son of the master, Charlie Bell. She may even be in love with him. Certainly he cares enough about her and the children that he steals them from his own father when he learns they are to be sold. They run together to the North. The narrator imagines that on the first morning of the run to freedom, Sybela realizes that she can walk away from Charlie and the children, away from responsibility. What she can-not escape is her own voice: "She could not leave it, or bury it and cry over it; she was nothing but that sound, and the sound was alone" (425). What gives her selfhood is not her relationship with the white man or their children; these are external, imposed aspects of her being. Her self-telling, her construction through internal speaking, is the core self. She creates herself as a subject in this moment, and this is the meaning of her freedom. In this act of creation, she becomes like Orion and Mother Belle. Whatever happens after this point cannot deprive her of this moment.

The meaning of the story and of *Damballah* as a whole can be understood in terms of this experience. The narrator describes his Aunt May's way of telling the family history as one in which stories are embedded within each other, each with its own value and place within the larger narrative. "What seems to ramble begins to cohere when the listener begins to understand the process, understands that the voice seeks to recover everything, that the voice proclaims *nothing is lost,* that the listener is not passive but lives like everything else within the story" (425). Sybela is both the first voice and the first listener. Her attention to her own experience makes all the later ones possible, including the versions of her own life.

The importance of this subjectivity is evident when the narrator brings his brother's experience into the story. When Tommy and Ruchell are captured, they are treated as spectacle, as "[b]ad dudes. Mean nigger men. Killers" (426). They are objects of the gaze of the crowd around the jail. They have no voices, only a bizarre celebrity. They escape objectification by refusing to look back, refusing in effect to see themselves in the staring eyes of others. The narrator understands this as a performance, as a way of satisfying the crowd without conceding its claims: "Everything about your faces disclaimed the accident that is happening to your bodies" (426). The narrator then imagines that Sybela would have behaved in much the same way, since if she had been captured, she too would have been paraded as an example of the black beast. Both of these instances, incorporating as they do spectacle, attempted humiliation, and incarceration, recall Mother Belle and her cage. The text seeks through both incident and imagery to create the connections across history the narrator initially saw as so important. The implication of the linkage is that one's inner strength exists to be drawn upon regardless of the conditions created by those who can control one's external being.

But access to this strength has to be a question, not a straightforward answer. The narrator interrogates himself: "Ask myself if I would have committed the crime of running away or if I would have stayed and tried to make the best of a hopeless situation" (427). In this framework, to be black and desirous of freedom is to be defined as criminal, regardless of time or circumstance. In this sense, Tommy's participation in a robbery-killing is secondary to a social order that defines him as guilty from birth on the basis of his skin color. He is caught in its gaze as the black monster that fascinates and horrifies simultaneously. His actual behavior only provides the legal sanction for a literal imprisonment that concretizes the spiritual and psychological one already in existence. His "crime" is being.

But Sybela's story and its meaning do not end with the claim of selfhood in defiance of the world. The story is also about endurance, about living in that world. When she and Charlie Bell finally arrive in Pittsburgh, they acquire land, only to be told that they are not welcome by whites in that neighborhood. They move to a more isolated area, where they raise 20 children and where other blacks then settle. Their original land is cursed, perhaps by Sybela, and Bell threatens anyone who touches his land. As May tells the story, it remained a troubled place well beyond Charlie's death. The black woman must "make a way out of no way" even in a land of so-called freedom.

Even this incident does not end the story, for May insists on carrying it forward into younger generations, members of whom she sees as directly in line with the ancestors. She is the one who actually saw Sybela, and she is the one who sees both the successes and the troubles of younger generations: " 'Hurts me to my heart. I remembers the babies. How beautiful they were. Then somebody tells me this one's dead, or that one's dying or Rashad going to court today or they gave Tommy Life' " (431). Thus the need for strength is still there. The power that the ancestors had, not to overcome but to endure in dignity, is needed as much as and perhaps even more than it was before.

One important way of finding that power is through telling the family's stories, both the weaknesses and the strengths. It becomes the narrator's value and purpose to record the stories and thus help to preserve the sense of group identity that in part makes endurance possible. Moreover, it is essential to keep alive the voices themselves because, as Sybela knew, the voice is the self. Wideman seeks through the short fictions of *Damballah* to retain not just the experiences, as either inspiration or warning, but also the experiencing selves. He does in literary terms what the figure of May does orally: he tries to make certain that "nothing is lost." This point is crucial because his understanding of American history is that it has sought to erase ordinary black voices and lives. The "gathering of the family" that is one of the functions of the god Damballah becomes a means of refusing that erasure and thus recovering one important part of history. In addition, those voices speak words of power; they bring the self into being and sustain not only that self but the generations to come. These "letters" to the imprisoned brother become, then, one effort to create spiritual connections that transcend physical conditions. Knowing what the ancestors have endured and how they survived provides an alternative narrative to the social definition of the black self and its fate. But as Lizabeth understands in "Solitary," it is not sufficient to have faith in what is outside, whether God or family. The journey outward to the past must return always to the inner self. The power of the ancestors is there, but it must be embraced and believed, not to escape the world but to live in it.

Fever: Storytelling
and the Quest for Meaning

The stories of *Fever* (1989) blend tradition and experimentation, the past and the present, history and fiction. In each story, Wideman reveals a postmodern sensibility by giving special attention to the problems of meaning and storytelling. He places in the foreground of several pieces the distinction between the classical short-story form and the practices of African-American storytelling. The extreme example of the postmodern is "Surfiction," a narrative that comments repeatedly on itself as an effort to create a story. It opens with a comment on a Charles Chesnutt tale; the commentary incorporates much contemporary language, then after several paragraphs turns to its own opening, which is identical to Chesnutt's. It then creates a dialogue between the narrator and the reader in which the reader is caught perusing the narrator's journal. Then the story begins again, but it quickly takes on a metafictional quality in the narrative of a professor teaching a husband and wife who keep diaries; the husband is also writing a novel that includes a character much like his wife. The professor reads their material (diaries and novel) while preparing a presentation on "surfiction." The narrative ends not with resolution of conflict but with a series of well-known lines (with variations) from masterpieces of fiction.

"Surfiction" could be seen simply as a tour de force that demonstrates the author's ability to do what other, better-known contemporary authors and critics do. But the reference to Chesnutt's manipulation of language as a black response to racial oppression suggests another layer of meaning to the story. Throughout both his short and long fiction, Wideman challenges formal literary traditions. But unlike white postmodernist writers, he does not assume that meaning can no longer be reliably communicated or that narrative has no relationship to reality. Rather, as he suggests in "Surfiction," "American, Western, twentieth century" culture has become so self-absorbed and disconnected from reality that it cannot address the significant issues of human experience. Within this cultural encoding process, "all goes swimmingly until a voice from the watermelon patch intrudes" (193). In this collection, and in his writing generally, Wideman seeks to be that voice. Thus "Surfiction" becomes a parody, an act of "signifying,"[3] on the alienating self-reflexive method of contemporary writing. For him, the significance of stories and storytelling is that they enable an exploration of the meaning of experience, especially its African-American aspects.

The Complexity of Storytelling

A narrative that emphasizes storytelling as process, and that reveals an underlying message only on reflection, is "Little Brother." The title figure is a dog owned by the family of the narrator. A footnote at the end of the collection identifies the story's source: "My wife and love of my life, to whom this story is dedicated, suggested that my Aunt Geraldine's strange dog needed a biographer" (266). The text consists of voices, with no authorial intrusion. The voices move from topic to topic, following the logic of memory and feeling rather than formal plot structure. Two sisters discuss life in the family home and the neighborhood, in both the past and the present. The dog is the touchstone for the conversation, the theme of which is love and loyalty. Geraldine describes Little Brother's sexual escapades but also his faithful return after a few days. This leads to discussion of human relationships, such as Geraldine's marriage to Ernie White, who was willing to wait years while she took care of her mother. Also commented on are the children's love for the mother, for each other, for the household pets, and for people in the neighborhood.

What keeps the story from becoming saccharine is the context of loss and death that shapes the talk. Geraldine was forced to choose between romance and family responsibility because of her mother's illness; only death enabled her marriage. Even many years later, she cannot answer her sister's question about whether she loved Ernie during those unmarried years. Penny herself has only a halfhearted reply when the question is turned back on her: "Penny. Did you love Billy? Five children. Twenty-seven years off and on before he jumped up and left for good. I must have. Some of the time" (237).

A young woman and her daughter, friends of Geraldine's, are the only white residents of the neighborhood. Their presence sometimes creates awkward situations that bode ill: "Saw her dressed up real nice in Sears in East Liberty last week and she ducked me. I know why, but it still hurt me. Like it hurts me to think my little sugar Carolyn will be calling people niggers someday. If she don't already" (237). A balance must be maintained between concern and affection for people and recognition of their limitations. The sisters are in a sense economic; they cannot afford extravagant emotions, such as strong romantic feelings for men whom they cannot have or who fail them. They do not expect much of young white women or the young black men who might accost them. They refuse sentimentality; wishing that things could be some other way wastes energy needed for caring for and about those around them. The world is a hostile place, and survival with integrity is a difficult task and is also the best that their lives offer.

The dog Little Brother serves as an emblem of their lives and their community. He refuses to enter the house apparently because Ote (the sisters' brother) called him a "scrawny rat" when Geraldine first brought him to the house. Ugly and rejected, he nonetheless remains loyal to the family. Even Ote eventually takes some responsibility for him by building a doghouse under the porch. The very insult that marginalizes Little Brother gives him a place in the family history. The symbolic significance is that among those who are on the margins of society and who can be insulted even by those they care about, there is a special responsibility to construct family wherever outsiders are found. Little Brother is what he is, but his identity increases rather than decreases his value in this narrative of invented family.

"Valaida," in contrast, is about the failure to construct family even when the desire is present. Another endnote to the collection explains that Valaida Snow was a jazz artist of the early and mid twentieth century who has been largely ignored despite her great talent. The premise of the story is that she saved a young Jewish boy from almost certain death in a concentration camp. Many years later in his New York apartment, Cohen, now a grown man, tries to tell his black housekeeper about the incident. The perspective is primarily his, though the narrative voice is third person.

The story opens, however, with the voice of Valaida Snow speaking from heaven to a former band member being interviewed by a music historian. She urges Bobby to make the story a good one that tells at least part of the truth, the part about her success as an artist. Here again Wideman comments on the process of storytelling, suggesting how the reader should understand the text. The truth, in the sense of historical reality, is secondary to the quality of the story. We are to measure the success of the artist, not the historian, in evaluating the material presented. In a tale making use of historical people and events, this is an important distinction.

But the story also immediately enters ethical territory. Another part of Valaida's experience is suffering and racism, about which not even Bobby knows everything. She herself was imprisoned in the camps and had to endure beatings and deprivation. She tells in this opening of trying to save the life of "a pitiful little stomped-down white boy" (166), but she does not know if he survived. Her story, then, is one of celebrity and great pain, which includes, incidentally, a gesture of unselfish heroism.

The scene and perspective shifts to Cohen, the boy who has become an old man. He of course remembers the camp incident quite differently. It is the central event in an otherwise uneventful life. Though he has been relatively successful, survival of the camps, especially with the aid of the black woman whom he never actually met, remains his defining experience. It also shapes, to some extent, his relationship with the maid, Clara Jackson. He has little ability for conversation with her, though she has worked for him for many years. His attitude suggests social (and perhaps racial) superiority, though she seems to dominate the space when she is present. He appears overly sensitive to her presence and experiences a feeling of displacement when she is around, despite her apparent indifference to him. He is oblivious to racial etiquette, referring to "colored" people though the story takes place in the late 1980s, and he is puzzled that she takes offense at his word choice.

He decides one day to tell Clara the story of the woman who saved him, though she is primarily interested in finishing her work so she can do her Christmas shopping. His desire to tell, to have her sit and listen, is so unusual that she is momentarily stopped in her tracks. He offers to make her tea, but she continues to worry over the vacuum cleaner, though listening politely. He then tells of the incident, calling Valaida "a dark angel who fell from the sky and saved me" (174). In the process of telling, he tries to create an identification between his benefactor and his housekeeper: "A woman like you. Many years ago. A lifetime ago. Young then as you would have been. And beautiful. As I believe you must have been, Mrs. Clara" (173).

He wishes to be understood as appreciating the role of black women in his life, but he defines their role in terms of what they have done for him, not who they are as people. Valaida saved his life, but he does not know her name; Clara provides order in his life, but he so thoroughly

37

sees her in her subservient role that for years he misses her obvious physical features. His description of her in the middle of the story reveals his self- centered reading:

> A tiny woman, no doubt about it. Lumpy now. Perhaps she steals and hides things under her dress. Lumpy, not fat. Her shoulders round and padded. Like the derelict women who live in the streets and wear their whole wardrobes winter spring summer fall. She has put on flesh for protection. To soften blows. To ease around corners. Something cushioned to lean against. Something to muffle the sound of bones breaking when she falls. A pillow for all the heads gone and gone to dust who still find ways at night to come to her and seek a resting place. He could find uses for it. Extra flesh on her bones was not excess, was a gift. The female abundance, her thickness, her bulk as reassuring as his hams shrink, his fingers become claws, the chicken neck frets away inside those razor-edged collars she scrubs and irons. (170)

He opens the description by imagining her as criminal, then as derelict, without any awareness that the roundness of her shoulders quite probably is caused by years of menial labor, such as scrubbing and ironing his shirts. The middle of the paragraph seems a moment of empathy, especially coming from one who has himself suffered blows and the deaths of loved ones. But then it becomes clear that her flesh exists for others, as a "pillow." Further, there is a Shylockian element in the statement "He could find uses for it. Extra flesh on her bones was not excess, was a gift." Her body, her being, has value in terms of its benefit to him. She is a pound of flesh that he lacks and can use.

Thus the meaning of black women to him is the sacrifice of their bodies for his. Given this perspective, it is not surprising that Clara offers little in the way of commentary: "Always thought it was just you people over there doing those terrible things to each other" (174). "You people" might be read as her insensitivity to centuries of Jewish persecution culminating in the Holocaust. But given the revelation of Cohen's attitudes toward blacks, which are not racism so much as a hurtful racial ignorance and even innocence, her phrase seems to carry the message that, when it comes to African Americans, Cohen is just another white man, whatever his personal history and suffering might be.

Through "Valaida," Wideman addresses the dynamics of black-Jewish relations. The suffering on both sides is real, but it is not the same. And the fact of suffering does not necessarily give one insight to or empathy for different experiences. Cohen wants Clara to be the emotional "pillow" for his old-age alienation, just as Valaida was the physical pillow in his childhood. But he has been so absorbed in his own very real pain that he has not noticed Clara's, some of which he has caused, not by design but by inattention. Thus the message is that suffering does not absolve us from responsibility, nor does it necessarily gain us the sympathy and human connection we may desire. The connection must be created, not assumed, and it must be done as much in the mundanity of life as in the extraordinary moments.

"Doc's Story" carries on the quest for comfort through story. In "Little Brother," the effort is made through family memory, and in "Valaida" it is made through narratives of suffering told by people who remain strangers to each other. In "Doc's Story," the central character seeks through a tale of the past some meaning for the present. His wife leaves him, for reasons that are not made clear; this obscurity suggests that those reasons are not the key issue of the story. He copes with the situation by joining the neighborhood basketball players who gather in the park every day. What interests him is not the ball-playing so much as the stories that are told before, between, and after games. Wideman very carefully establishes the context for storytelling, thereby indicating its ritual significance and its particular importance for the focal character: "He collects the stories they tell. He needs a story now. The right one now to get him through this long winter because she's gone and won't leave him alone" (146). Thus he assumes and seeks the sustaining and curative powers of narrative, much as earlier generations had used the blues to express and contain their troubles.

The context of neighborhood, intoxicants, narrative practices, and games creates an order that is lacking in his emotional life. This structure is evident despite the grittiness and seeming failure represented by the context; these are men with little else to do in their lives in a decaying community and who can afford only cheap wine. But the world generated by the stories is one full of interesting characters and social commentary. The most important tales are about Doc, who is somehow central to all the storytelling:

> Of all the stories, the one about Doc had bothered him most. Its orbit was unpredictable. Twice in one week, then only once more last summer. He'd only heard Doc's story three times, but that was enough to establish Doc behind and between the words of all the other stories. In a strange way Doc presided over the court. You didn't need to mention him. He was just there. Regent Park stories began with Doc and ended

39

with Doc and everything in between was preparation, proof the circle
was unbroken. (147)

This paragraph suggests the folkloric aspect of "Doc's Story." The tale
is told several times, but no one considers such repetition inappropri-
ate; in fact, the meaning of the story for this community of men requires
such ritualization, for communal values must be regularly reaffirmed.
Folk community is further emphasized in the fact that Doc does not
always have to be mentioned explicitly; he is so much a part of the
group sensibility that he operates as a presiding and informing spirit
even when he is not named.

Despite Doc's thoroughgoing connection with this group, what gives
him heroic status in some ways is his difference from them. He had not
only played ball at the university; he had taught there. What is noteworthy in the tales about him is not so much this intellectual achievement but the fact that whites at the institution had a hard time believing that he could be anything other than a coach. His response to this
was laughter, a response that to the black men telling and hearing the
story seems courageous. It is a refusal to be defeated by racism, even
while recognizing its omnipresence. Moreover, Doc regularly invites the
players to his house in a white neighborhood, despite the obvious dis-
pleasure of his neighbors. He thus affirms his race in the public sphere,
without any note of condescension, and thereby validates the communal sense of black male identity in a way that none of the others have an
opportunity to do.

Added to this specialness is the fact of his blindness, which came on
gradually. Because Doc had been one of the best of the players, the
change in his condition was potentially devastating. However, he
seemed to adapt by shooting foul shots with great accuracy. He prac-
ticed at night, and he came to the games with his usual quick wit and
neighborhood knowledge. In one story about him, one day things
change for Doc, for reasons the storyteller does not pretend to understand. Doc begins to miss his foul shots, and one of the young kids grabs
an errant shot and dunks it. Instead of joining the celebration, Doc
takes offense; because of their respect for him, the others are extremely
uncomfortable. Then he insists on playing in a game, a demand the others cannot refuse given his status in the group. The outcome of the
game and his performance in it are of little significance to the teller of
the tale; Doc's playing itself is the crucial event. At the same time, it is
important to the story's meaning that Doc does not embarrass himself.

This is not a tale of the mighty fallen into humiliation, nor is it a sentimental tale of success against all odds.

The central character, having heard the narrative, chooses to apply it to his personal life. It is a story he would like to tell his ex-wife, a story of possibility: *"If a blind man could play basketball, surely we ..."* (153). But it is important to go back to the character's initial thought that "of all the stories, the one about Doc had bothered him most" (147). Two things are bothersome: his ex-wife's attitude toward African-American narratives and the underlying meaning of Doc's story. She understands the narratives as the "pathology of the oppressed" when he tries to tell her the tales of flying Africans, of shape changers, and of conjurers: "She listened intently, not because she thought she'd hear the truth. For her, belief in magic was like belief in God. Nice work if you could get it" (152). Precisely because he understands the story of Doc as magical, it is doubtful that she would be able to take it seriously. Her skepticism is one of the qualities he admires, but it is a quality that inhibits the belief needed to be a member of a folk community.

Furthermore, the main character's effort to find a functional aspect to the story by making it a device with which to pursue and persuade his ex-wife may well be frustrated by the narrative's ambiguity. When the story is told for itself, its inherent mystery is part of the experience. But the effort to impose a clear meaning invites skepticism. After all, the story can be read as an instance of denial, as Doc refuses to accept that he can no longer be the player he was. His rudeness to the young player indicates a psychological struggle with his new identity as a blind man. In this sense, the tale can be read as pathetic rather than heroic. Moreover, neither readers nor the focal character learn what happened to Doc; he seems to have disappeared after the events described. The potential message of that fact is that sometimes things are simply over, surviving only as memory and story. One word the character repeatedly uses in describing his wife is "perfect," but Doc's story is about imperfection—mischance, frustration, loss of selfhood. The central character's belief in the story indicates a belief in life's imperfections; this faith precludes a relationship with a "perfect" woman.

Thus "Doc's Story" examines the value and limitations of storytelling. Narrative offers the possibility of community, but it requires belief in the "magic" that it creates. In a sense, Wideman is exploring here the human significance of a suspension of disbelief. That suspension demands not only acceptance of content but also acceptance of the process by which mystery and ambiguity are created. To refuse belief, to simplify meaning, or to seek only usefulness is to reject the power of story.

Given the nature of Wideman's fiction, both short and long, with its emphasis on moral, social, and political issues and its frequent reliance on personal history, the distinction between story and simple parable is important. His work often seems to present itself as allegory or direct statement rather than as multilayered fiction. "Valaida" or "Tommy" from *Damballah*, for example, can easily be read as social comment on racism or on the problems of young black men. In "Doc's Story," Wideman is warning against such an interpretation. The characters are not to be understood as ciphers for moral or sociological analysis. It is the voices, the memories, the struggles that are important to acknowledge. In these stories and in those that are constructed around them there is the potential for complex human meaning that cannot be reduced to direct statement. Wideman often does not even attempt an articulation of that meaning. Instead, he relies on the "magic" of storytelling and on the possibility of a constructed community of believers in that magic. He often makes moral positions within the text quite clear but does not reduce the characters to fit those values. Thus he creates open-ended tales that express a desire for moral order but are skeptical about its achievement.

Blues Narratives

"When It's Time to Go" and the subsequent story "Presents" can be read as blues narratives in that they offer stories of the troubles of black men told primarily through their voices. In this sense, they are related to "Doc's Story" and, in a less direct way, to "Valaida." They are concerned with the vicissitudes of life, the chance alterations between fortune and disaster, happiness and sorrow. Neither focuses primarily on racial or sexual conflict. Rather, they are about the need to tell one's experience, to make sense of it through story. In them, the "fever" of the book's title is expressed through the compulsion to explain even to a stranger and thus have one's voice heard.

"When It's Time to Go" takes the form of a standard narrative, that of the handicapped artist. In such a tale, one is told the source of the disability, the struggles of the child, the gradual achievement of mastery, and the accomplished artistry. Within the African-American community, the form has often been used to tell of the blind bluesmen of the early twentieth century, but the pattern is also a classic black narrative of success against the odds. It serves to validate an individualistic "bootstraps" ideology of hard work and ambition.

Given Wideman's postmodern and critical perspective, it is not surprising that he subverts this master narrative in the process of using it. The story opens with a briefly suggested frame in which the narrator agrees to listen to a story. Thus he immediately positions himself as audience, not speaker. The storyteller takes over until near the end of the tale. This inside speaker primarily uses the third person to tell about a blind boy from Alabama. The story is a strange one, with ghosts, magic, and special powers. He opens with "Once upon a time" to create the space for these mysterious elements.

But the story is in no sense a simple folktale; rather, it contains elements of harsh realism. The "ghost" is the father, a less-than-reliable husband:

> Little boy's daddy was a shadow like that and he told Clara he loved her and gave her a baby behind him swearing how beautiful she was and how much he loved her and rubbing her big butt and telling her he'd stay with her always. Well, he came up a little short on the always. (205)

This fatherless child comes into the world with other problems that also mark him as different. He is born with a caul, a piece of placenta that in folk tradition often signifies magical qualities, including, ironically for this story, second sight. In this instance, the caul nearly strangles him and may contribute to his blindness. Despite the handicap, the child quickly takes on nearly legendary status. He learns to talk very early and, even though blind, has striking eyes: "Them long eyes look right through you but can't see a thing. Some say they was green and some say they was lavender. Some say you could hear that child's eyes crackle you get close enough" (206).

The specialness increases when he begins to see first light, then the outline of objects. The storyteller meditates on the value of gaining sight, especially if, as he notes, one is doomed to lose it again. A theme of ambivalence is introduced: is gaining and then losing something a blessing or a curse? One has the memory, but it is a memory of loss. The question is important in this case because the child's sight begins slowly to fail. He links his loss to a recurring dream of his father running away. The narrative in this sense repeats Wideman's frequent motif of the desire for and loss of the father.

Part 1

In this story, father figures are consistently assigned blame. The best doctor in the community will not treat black patients, and so Clara must take her son to the one who "treated anybody he got that whiskey on his breath and them yellow cake teeth people got to turn they face away and he's thinking like it's respect or some dumb scared rabbit coon fraid to look him in the eye. Old Mr. Shitbreath Doctor, he don't know squat" (207). The narrator clearly holds these two medical men responsible for the child's deteriorating condition. They may be authority figures, but their racism and indifference cause great harm. Like the biological father, they offer nothing to the son.

Clara, devoted to her child, follows the alcoholic doctor's advice, though it causes the child great pain. Crusts keep forming over his eyes, and she must place boiling hot rags over them until the crust softens and can be peeled away. The text goes into great detail about the process:

> [He] wrings them boiling rags and lays them on his eyes. Hot as he can stand it, hot enough to suck all the color out his skin, so it's bleached like side meat been cooking all day. He a tough little monkey and scared too so he lays them on hot as he can stand it. Thinks of fire. Thinks he got to burn to see. His eyeballs burning like they up there in the sky, in the fire colors of sunset. He sits blind as a bat with them hot pads over his eyes and tries to think of things take his mind off the scalding, till the crust gets soft and sticky like candy. (208)

Such intense pain takes on a quality of torture when it is evident that the effort has no medical value. This narrative moves beyond "Doc's Story" in that it adds physical experience to the psychological effects of blindness. It also hints at the motif of fever that shapes the title story. One of the disturbing aspects of the story is that the mother continues the torment out of her desperate belief that something must be done. Her neighbors believe that she is in fact a witch and so wonder why she does not take matters into her own hands:

> Some the younger sassy ones asking if Clara so bad why don't she cure her blind child her own bad self. Why she trotting way down the road to that whiskey-head quack she so bad. Well, there's some people you can't tell nothing to anyway. . . . It's more than one kind of power in the world. Ain't no kind of power can win all the time. If one thing don't work don't be too proud to try something else. Clara loved her boy. Maybe she loved him so much she touch him and ain't no magic in

44

her hands ain't nothing but a natural woman when she touch him cause she love him so much. (208).

The story does not question Clara's "magic"; rather, it poses what might be called a blues dilemma. Love may in fact be disempowering. When it matters most, love may produce doubts that the power is great enough. If it does not work, then the guilt will be too great. Better to trust other sources, ones validated by the dominant community. But these sources may be indifferent or incompetent, as in this case, and the result will be heart-wrenching failure.

The teller of the tale calls the boy Sambo. The name serves to suggest not the racial stereotype but rather a postmodern black everyman. Sambo is the projected image of the dominant society and the one clearly believed by the doctors of the story. The child has no value or identity to them distinct from their projections. The narrative takes the reader past the image to the suffering child. This Little Black Sambo lives a difficult, painful, frustrated life instead of one of simple, natural pleasure. The name challenges the assumptions of white society by forcing a reassessment of racial designation. The effect is heightened when the narrator suddenly shifts to the first person. We learn that *he* is Sambo and still resents what was done to him. He has become a piano player in bars and makes his own way in life, despite often literally stumbling. But he has no self-pity: "Ain't never felt sorry for myself neither cause my mama never did and I know she love me better than I love myself" (210).

The frame narrator reenters the text in order to bear witness to the storytelling. He serves to authenticate Sambo's tale not by certifying its claims of fact but rather by naming the context in which the telling takes place. In this bar, at this time of night, with these people, truth is told. Moreover, the reader will believe it as well because the reader has been in the same place:

> So what you are saying you sort of say to anybody who cares to listen because you're saying it mostly to yourself. Hey. You know what I mean. You been there, ain't you sisters and brothers. In the Crawford Grill at three-thirty in the morning on barstools rapping. (211)

Sambo's story is true for all those who can be called "sisters and brothers."

The blind man's voice takes on a philosophical quality at the end as it joins that of the frame narrator. He wonders about the value of sight, since, in his experience, sight paradoxically produces a lack of attention. Those who can see do not have to notice the world because they take it for granted. "Eyes get to be like them dogs lead blind people around. They do the seeing and you just follow along behind" (211). Seeing is a form of blindness, and for Sambo it is also treacherous. All of us, according to him, are "steady losing the light," and if we do not pay attention we will not know what we have really seen when the darkness comes. The frame narrator extends the point by inviting readers to imagine their blood entering the body of the piano player and then to close their eyes and try to "remember the color of light" (212). The story of an unfortunate child becomes the story of all through a series of narrative shifts.

This transformative action of storytelling also includes the metaphorical significance of the tale. Blindness serves as a way to talk about race. This is perhaps the deeper meaning of the name Sambo. What the character must experience is a condition over which he has no control. Sambo is not certain whether the blindness is itself a bad thing; what he does know is that the indifference and malpractice of the doctors make his life much worse. His childhood is filled with pain and false promises. Only when his condition is accepted does he find the strength, talent, and attentiveness needed to survive in a world filled with obstacles. In this sense, blindness, like blackness, is a circumstance, not a handicap. The very limits it imposes (or that the world imposes because of it) may produce insights not otherwise available.

By this reading, to be black is neither good nor bad in itself; it is simply a fact of life. What matters is what others do with that fact and what the self does with it. The "handicap" quality of it is constructed by those who assume it is a deprivation. Those who are antagonistic or who offer careless advice create problems. Within the circumstance itself, there may in fact be a certain power or understanding that others lack. Thus the story becomes a parable of American race relations that invites resolution through its invitation to readers to imagine themselves to be like Sambo and thus more attentive to the world.

"Presents" attempts to be a sentimental and religious narrative but functions instead as a blues story. The narrative shifts frequently and easily between first person and free indirect discourse, blended with unassigned dialogue. This shifting of voices creates a dis-ease in the text consistent with the ambiguity of the tale. Through these devices, Wideman effectively disrupts what is labeled a "simple" story.

The plot may in fact be called simple. A young boy lives with his much-beloved grandmother, Big Mama. On Christmas Eve, she gives him a used guitar and says that he has to learn how to play on his own. He then offers his gift, a song he has made up especially for her. After he sings it, she predicts his life, stating that it will involve great success and humiliating failure. By the next morning, Christmas Day, she has died. He goes on to become a musician and shifts repeatedly between religious and blues performance. At this level, the story is, in effect, O. Henry without the irony. Much of the text is given over to the loving interaction between child and woman. It is a sentimental tale often told by the narrator when he "preaches."

But from early in the narrative, the story subverts itself. It opens with the memory of Big Mama's voice, which the speaker claims to hear despite the fact that she died many years earlier. She is an absent presence that he cannot quite locate. Time is also fluid in the text; although the story opens in the present, the narrative slips back and forth:

> Big Mama. Big Mama. Doubling her not because she is not real enough once but because her life takes up so much space. I stare at her afraid to look away. Scared she'll be gone if I do. Scared I'll be gone. (218)

The voice opening the passage seems that of an adult speaker, whereas at the end it is childlike. What is also suggested is the speaker's deep dependence on his grandmother; his very existence requires her presence. Immediately after this intensely personal comment, the speaker is viewed from the outside: "He is saucer-eyed. Awkward. A big, nappy head" (218). The narrative voice is self-fragmenting, as it moves among dialogue, objective comment, and first-person and limited third-person narration. Such variation implies the speaker's problem in finding a way to tell this "simple" tale. The difficulty involves at some level the persona the narrator is willing to accept for himself. The simple story is a lie in the light of the man he has become. Yet he is unwilling to let go of his childlike belief in the love of Big Mama; it seems to be his only counter to total despair.

The significance of the latter point is evident in his memory of his life with her. There is an almost literal return to the womb: "In her lap he will curl and sleep and always find soft room to snuggle deeper. To fall. To sleep" (219). Her body is the space of absolute security. None of the unarticulated anxiety of separation from his parents can reach him in such a space. Though seven years old at the time of this experience, he exists almost in utero. This sense is reinforced by his description of being under her bed, where it is quiet and safe. Since this incident is positioned shortly before her death, the loss takes the form of separation trauma. Thus the memory of the most secure and comforting moment of his life is accompanied by a tremendous sense of loss.

The gift of the guitar only adds to the complexity of the story. It has been hidden under the bed, thus sharing his womblike space. When it is brought out, it is "swaddled" in an old blanket. The language shifts from imagery of birth (perhaps even of Christ) to that of sensuality:

> Then Big Mama digs into folds and flaps, uncovers woman curves, the taut shaft. There are long strings and a hole in the center. Gently as she goes she cannot help accidents that trick stirrings from the instrument. A bowl of jelly quivering. Perhaps all it needs is the play of her breath as she bends over it, serious and quiet as a child undressing a doll. Or the air all by its ownself is enough to agitate the strings when Big Mama finally has laid it bare across her bed. (219)

The blend of adult and child, of male and female imagery implies that the guitar is much more than a simple object to the speaker. It is simultaneously sibling, mother, and father, with all the psychological possibilities those terms imply. Since this is the language of the remembering adult, later associations appear to be read back into this moment of "simple" gift giving.

The generosity of her present, to which he responds in innocence not only with joy but also with song, is then qualified by her foretelling of his life. In doing so, she robs him of innocence and purity, since the story requires a knowledge of good and evil:

> Then she lays out the sad tale of his life as a man. He'll rise in the world, sing for kings and queens but his gift for music will also drag him down to the depths of hell. She tells it gently, he is only a boy, with her eyes fixed on the ceiling and they fill up with tears. Oh yes. Oh yes, yes. Yes, Jesus. The life he must lead a secret pouring out of her. Emptying her. Already she's paying for the good and evil in him. (220)

This narrative, though told gently, becomes his troubled fate. In the present-time telling, he has experienced what she predicted. The question is whether her telling was a gift or a curse. Unable to answer that question, the narrator is doomed to telling the story until he can resolve the issue. And as shall be seen, because of this uncertainty the guitar, apparently so generously given, is implicated in his troubles.

But even these uncertainties do not represent the full complexity. The one purity in the text—the boy's innocence—is itself called into doubt. The narrator confesses to once having watched his mother take a bath from his safe hiding place under the bed. His voyeurism is quite deliberate and associated with guilt: "She has a big, round behind with hairs at the bottom. He thinks of watermelons and can't eat that fruit without guilt ever after" (220). Only his fear of discovery prevents his seeing her full nakedness as she turns to face the bed. But his language suggests that he knows what he would see: "Titties. Pussycat between her legs" (221). The childlike diction implies knowledge contrary to simple innocence. Little wonder that he comments, "The story has more skins than an onion. And like an onion it can cause a grown man to cry when he starts peeling it" (221).

The eroticized environment suggests a narrator aware of his own oedipal desires but unable to satisfy, suppress, or resolve them. In the absence of the father, he cannot quite escape the space of the feminine and thus cannot truly take possession of his own life. In this sense, the guitar becomes the emblem of his ambiguity. Though a gift to him, he doubts that it can ever truly be his:

> Where did she find a guitar? Who'd played the instrument before it was his? Could it ever be his if other fingers had plucked the strings, run up and down the long neck? Grease and sweat ground into its wood, its metal strings. When he was at last alone with the gift she'd given him and told him not to play till Christmas, he'd peered into the hole in its belly. Held it by its fat hips and shook it to hear if anybody'd left money in there. (222)

He is always too late. Some better musician has been here before him, like the lovers of the women in his life. He must always be the son of unknown fathers, whether biological or musical, and he must always deal with what they have left behind.

His fate is tied to the guitar. His grandmother provides him with the instrument by which his destiny is determined, and consistent with the ambiguity of that gift, he moves between the Lord's music and the devil's. He can never decide which of them is his true Father and thus tries to do the bidding of both. Though his grandmother had her clear preference, the guilt associated with her house and the doom forecast in her narrative problematizes the legacy. Not even breaking the guitar over his knee, which finally enables him to mourn for her after many years, rids him of his fate. He still must alternate between achieving fame and money and finding himself lying in his own vomit in the gutter.

As the man telling the story to a stranger, he cannot yet figure out why he must always end in the gutter. The story is ultimately a mystery, even to the teller. And because the narrative is his life, he can only go on living out the apparently meaningless pattern. Unlike Sambo of "When It's Time to Go," he cannot even offer some insight into what has happened to him. Instead he has only a pathetic desire: "Big Mama is where she is. He is here. Her voice plain as day in his ear. He wishes someone would pat him on his head and say everything's gon be all right" (224).

In these two stories Wideman explores the narrative possibilities of blues. They reflect the music's emphasis on the feeling of trouble in life, whatever form that might take. The point is to find a structure that will express that feeling so that subjective experience can be transmitted to the reader/audience. The point is not to resolve the difficulty so much as to express it. The teller succeeds to the extent that he can engage the audience in his narrative; he achieves control, not over his life but over the story of that life. And this, we are invited to believe, is the fate of everyone.

The Fever of History

The title story of *Fever* is the most complex in working through these principles. Wideman calls it a "meditation on history." By "history" he means not only the events but also the recording of those events. His narrative revises the historical record by invoking voices largely ignored in the construction of the past. The most important of these voices for this narrative is that of Richard Allen, the African-American minister who established the African Methodist Episcopal Church. The story is set in Philadelphia in 1793, the year of a yellow fever epidemic. From the beginning of the story, however, "fever" serves as a metaphor for America's "disease" of racism. A key source for the story is Allen's 1794 *Narrative*, written in large part to repudiate the charges that blacks had brought the fever to the city but were immune to it. The accusation makes them doubly criminal and also carefully evades white culpability. The disease seems to have been brought in on slave ships from the Caribbean, meaning of course that its African carriers had no choice about their destination. Nor is there evidence of any racial immunity to the horrifying effects of the fever; it is simply that most blacks in the city are segregated into the worst housing in the worst areas and thereby are not visible to most whites. What is presented as the official history is in fact a racist construction that serves primarily to validate its own prejudices. To understand the reality, it is necessary to listen to the "criminal" voice.

Allen works with Doctor Benjamin Rush, who not only cares for the dying and the dead but also performs autopsies to try to determine the cause of the disease. Allen is often the target of invective and even assault when he visits the homes of whites; neither their impending deaths nor his compassionate care protects him from racial insult. After finishing a day's work with Rush, Allen goes to the hovels and even caves of poor blacks, places no one else is willing to go. Here, in contradiction to the accusation against the race, he finds men, women, and children dying in the most wretched of circumstances, with no hope of a doctor's care. Allen's movement back and forth between whites and blacks, which emphasizes the commonality of symptoms and suffering but vast differences in conditions and treatment, point to the greater underlying disorder of racism.

Ironically, a different narrative voice indirectly reasserts the blame for the disease. From the consciousness of a slave on the Middle Passage, we learn of his being bitten by the Aëdes mosquito, the carrier of the fever. But of course it is the slave trade and not individual choice that has placed this unnamed man in his situation. In fact, part of the revision of history the story undertakes is that the victims become the criminals. As Allen understands, the real source of the fever is spiritual and moral:

> To explain the fever we need no boatloads of refugees, ragged and wracked with killing fevers, bringing death to our shores. We have bred the affliction within our breasts. Each solitary heart contains all the world's tribes, and its precarious dance echoes the drum's thunder. We are our ancestors and our children, neighbors and strangers to ourselves. Fever descends when the waters that connect us are clogged with filth. . . . Fever grows in the secret places of our hearts, planted there when one of us decided to sell one of us to another. (242–43)

This spiritual reading is set against the objective, scientific information about the mosquito and the findings of the autopsies, and the graphic descriptions of suffering and death. For the principal narrator, such a materialist interpretation of events is inadequate, as is the racist one. Such perspectives offer little in the way of understanding the forces of history. The materialist view, that the fever is caused simply by the mosquito (or, in Rush's imperfect science, by something in the body), ignores human responsibility. The racist view is all too eager to assign responsibility but does so out of hatred and greed. It is only a moral and spiritual view, which suggests ironically that Rush is right in looking inward, though not to the body, that explains that the material conditions are themselves the product of choices and acts of inhumanity that turn back on the perpetrators. Thus the fever is a product of human culture just as surely as it is a biological phenomenon. That it attacks across all boundaries—race, class, gender—suggests the unpredictable effects of human belief and action. They cannot be contained or explained by either science or ideology.

This larger moral view is also necessary to explain Allen himself. Master Abraham, a sick elderly Jewish merchant, asks why the black man stays to help the whites who abuse him. In their conversations, he repeatedly asks why Allen does not flee, why he does not go to his family. He wants to know why he serves as Rush's "lapdog" when he is clearly a man of great talent. He sees clearly a racial attitude toward blacks that matches the hatred of Jews in the European ghettos. Finally, he asserts that Allen fears his own freedom, preferring subservience and busyness to searching for and claiming his own place in the world. In other words, he accuses the black man of having a slave mentality even though he is physically free.

If Allen's interpretation of the underlying causes of the disorder are correct, then neither subservience nor even self-sacrificing Christian duty is adequate to explain him. If the real cause of the disease is the clogging of human connections, with the "filth" of greed, racism, arrogance, and dishonesty, then the only way to save both the self and the community is through sympathy, nurture, and contact. Allen does what he can, even though it is so little: his family dies, and only the arrival of cold weather stops the fever. In fact, Wideman goes further to suggest that the city never really recovers from its "fever." The penultimate paragraph in the story blends past and present:

> Only a handful of deaths the last weeks of November. The city was recovering. Commerce thriving. Philadelphia must be revictualed,

refueled, reconnected to the countryside. . . . A new century would soon be dawning. We must forget the horrors. The Mayor proclaims a new day. Says let's put the past behind us. Of the eleven who died in the fire he said extreme measures were necessary as we cleansed ourselves of disruptive influences. The cost could have been much higher, he said I regret the loss of life, especially the half dozen kids, but I commend all city officials, all volunteers who helped return the city to the arc of glory that is its proper destiny. (265)

The fire referred to is the MOVE bombing and conflagration that occurred in 1985. MOVE was a black radical group that the city was determined to eliminate, even though the mayor and other important officials were black themselves. The bomb police dropped on the house killed the people inside, including children, and destroyed by fire much of the neighborhood. Wideman offers a detailed account of the incident in the novel *Philadelphia Fire* (1990). In "Fever," his blending of past and present suggests the continuity of spiritual disease. A city willing to both blame and sacrifice members of the community because they are different is a city destroying itself from the inside. And as the epigraph from Robert Morris (1777) indicates, Philadelphia is "to the United States what the heart is to the human body in circulating the blood" (239). Thus Wideman creates a complex network of figuration in order to make his social and moral criticism. The Philadelphia of the 1790s serves as metaphor for the contemporary city; the city is synecdoche for the nation. What binds them is the spiritual disorder that permits exploitation and abuse of the most needy members of the community and that includes a willful blindness to the self destructiveness of such behavior. The problem is not simply one of racism, as the MOVE disaster shows. It is the arrogance and indifference bred by the pursuit and exercise of power.

The healthful option is Richard Allen, who cannot remain indifferent. Partway through the story, as part of Wideman's postmodern technique of mixing modes of discourse, an autopsy is described in considerable medical detail. At the end of the story, the narrator imagines a similar operation when Allen dies:

> When they cut him open, the one who decided to stay, to be a beacon and steadfast, they will find: Liver (1,720 grams), spleen (150 grams), right kidney (190 grams), left kidney (180 grams), brain (1,450 grams), heart (380 grams), and right next to his heart, the miniature hand of a child, frozen in a grasping gesture, fingers like hard tongues of flame,

still reaching for the marvel of the beating heart, fascinated still, though the heart is cold, beats not, the hand as curious about this infinite stillness as it was about thump and beat and quickness. (265)

The statistics are the same as those found in the earlier description, suggesting that Allen is like all of us; there is no difference based on race or any other physical or social factor. But this egalitarian assertion, which one would expect, also carries another meaning. There is no evidence of an intrinsic moral superiority; all have the same capacity for goodness.

The difference, of course, is the image of the child's hand, which echoes the image in Nathaniel Hawthorne's "The Birthmark" and which has a similar significance. It represents a common humanity, one too often ignored or repudiated in pursuit of individual or ideological goals. The two authors see this repudiation from different angles—Hawthorne from the quest for perfection and Wideman from historical suffering—but they share a desire to make that common humanity the moral center of human action and thought. The child's hand in "Fever," anthropomorphized as "fascinated" and "curious," symbolizes the position of Wideman's desired reader as in awe of the heroism of Richard Allen, driven to use his suffering and persecuted life for the common good. Not even the pattern of history, which seems to cast doubt on the effectiveness of such efforts, can overshadow their meaning. And because he is like us, there is hope even in the grip of our own "fever."

The stories of *Fever* can all be said to concern disease/dis-ease. From the commentary of "Surfiction" on contemporary culture and the emphasis in "Valaida" on failed communication to the blindness, frustration, and lost relationships of "Doc's Story," the entire collection presents struggles to deal with the world's disorder and suffering. Although in some cases the difficulties appear merely personal, Wideman variously shows that they represent larger cultural and political concerns. And where they are primarily social, as in "Fever," he directs us as well to the individual impact of ideologies and actions. By using some postmodern techniques—mixing of discourses, shifting of time, unreliable narration, blending of fact and fiction—he is able to construct moral tales without depending on a conventional moral order. His morality is an existential one that insists that individual efforts can be meaningful, valuable, and courageous even if unsuccessful. From his perspective, one purpose of storytelling is to keep alive such heroic tales, especially if they are the tales of the silenced and neglected. His particular concern is the narratives of African Americans, who are not history's chosen people in the sense of any superiority but rather its reluctant victims. In this role, as a group and as individuals, they symbolize the suffering and heroism of all humanity. Wideman takes a strong moral position in *Fever*, believing that such suffering should be exposed and ended but lacking optimism that it will.

Voices from Beyond: *All Stories Are True*

Some of the stories in *All Stories Are True* (1992) continue the concern with family and personal history, whereas others develop the experimental potential of other voices. In the five pieces selected for discussion—"All Stories Are True," "Everybody Knew Bubba Riff," "Backseat," "Newborn Thrown in Trash and Dies," and "Signs"—much of the narrative consists of interior monologues and personal memories. At the same time, each story expands outward to consider some aspect of the public realm, including prison life, child abuse, racism, politics, and sexuality. Comments on media, education, and urban decay are also incorporated. With these stories, Wideman further loosens the short-story form; his style is, depending on one's perspective, a postmodernist one of pastiche or the digressive and associational one of traditional (folk) storytelling. Perhaps the best way to describe his method is to think of it as the intersection of the two modes for the purpose of bringing together a variety of concerns. He has available a range of narrative strategies not limited by commitment to just one method. In his hands, versions of folk narration accommodate postmodern issues, and postmodern techniques, as in "Newborn," are made to resemble traditional storytelling.

"All Stories Are True"

The title story of the collection returns to Homewood in 1991. The narrator is a middle-aged man visiting his mother in the family home. He immediately sets up a connection between the local geography and the shape of memory. The names of the streets are a "litany" that brings back memories of the people and events associated with them. Homewood becomes a sacred, ritual space for him and also, he understands, for his mother: "[She] is listening to time, time voiced in no manmade measurements of days or minutes or years, time playing as it always must, background or foreground or taking up all the space we have, a tape of the street names chanted that releases every Homewood footstep she's ever heard or dreamed" (4). A tree symbolizes the endurance and character of the neighborhood:

> A massive tree centuries old holds out against the odds here across from my mother's house, one of the biggest trees in Pittsburgh, anchored in a green tangle of weeds and bushes, trunk thick as a Buick, black as night after rain soaks its striated hide. Huge spread of its branches canopies the foot of the hill where the streets come together. . . . As big as it is, its roots must run under her cellar. The sound of it drinking, lapping nourishment deep underground is part of the quiet when her house is empty. How the tree survived a city growing around it is a mystery. (4–5)

The tree can easily be read as the emblem of the black community in its survival, strength, and undeniable presence.

But this is not a nostalgic story. The poetic language and sacred space are intended to contrast with the harsh realities of the present. The mother proceeds to tell the story of a petty thief who, "just before Easter," went through the neighborhood and stole pots of flowers off porches and then the next day sold the plants without pots on a street corner. Both the pettiness and the arrogance of the theft suggest the fragility and decay of the neighborhood in contrast to the powerful tree.

The mother's account of the crime is followed by her narrative of her neighbor Wade, who in a single year saw both his wife and his dog die and who accidentally killed a neighborhood child. But the pathos of Wade's story leads to a reassertion of the mother's religious faith. The events in Wade's life could have led him to despair and a sense of meaninglessness, but instead his endurance reminds her of Job and thus renews her belief. Moreover, the connection affirms racial pride: "I did think of Job more than once when I prayed for Wade. And I guess Job surely did have Wade's face, and Wade's face, God bless him, surely isn't white" (9). This point is blended in an associational manner, consistent with oral tradition, into a conversation about the imprisoned brother and his new Muslim beliefs. Related to this are the tribulations he must face, including continued rejection of his appeal to the parole board. Thus the narratives of crime and trouble, of family and community that made up the first half of the story serve to set up the second half, in which the narrator visits his brother in prison.

The second half uses a language that is much harsher and more obscene, consistent with its representation of prison life. The intensity of the sunlight and heat is implicitly contrasted with the effects of the giant tree in Homewood. The brother has prematurely aged and has developed a deeply cynical view of the system that imprisons him. He acknowledges his own deeply flawed character but primarily tells stories of official cruelty and manipulation. The crucial anecdote involves the denial of his commutation request:

> [They] know I'm on pins and needles every minute of every day since I filed my commutation papers, but don't nobody say one god-blessed single solitary word good or bad for three months. I'm going crazy with the waiting. And too scared to ask anybody what's happening cause you know how that works. Ask a question and they say no just to spite you, just to get you out their face. (11–12)

Then, while waiting for a visit from his wife and baby, he receives a call that coldly informs him of the negative decision.

It is the sadistic character of the process that he draws attention to. The system seems specifically designed to produce dehumanization; there is no evidence of efforts toward rehabilitation or moral development:

> My own fault I'm here. I know I done some bad things. I'm in here, man, doing my time. Uh huh. Hard time. Lots of time for doing wrong. But they treat us like dog shit in here and that's wrong too. Guys get killed in here. Go crazy. But nobody cares. Long as they keep us locked up so they can do us anyway they want. Figure we in here, so they don't owe us nothing. But wrong is wrong, ain't it. Just cause we down, is it right to keep on kicking us. Guys get meaner and crazier in here. Every day you see the ones can't take it slipping further and further off. Distance in their eyes, bro. Ain't nobody home in them eyes. They shuffle around here like ghosts. Stop speaking to people. Stop keeping themselves clean. Gone, man. If you been around here any length of time you seen it happen to a lot of guys. You understand how easy it is to tune out and drop off the edge into your own little world. Another planet. You see why guys go off. Why they so cold and mean if they ever hit the street again. (13)

The argument against corrections policies and practices is carried here by the psychological mini-narrative of the statement. Rather than criminological data, he offers the cumulative mental and sensory effects of prison life. He presents images of ghosts, aliens, and sociopaths created by that life. His own response to the rejection of his appeal—"My life was over"—is simply one episode in the larger story of dehumanization.

A crucial part of the narrative is his resistance to that dehumanization. The story is one of enlightenment. He entered prison determined to be a "stone outlaw," to keep the guards and officials in fear of the violence of the inmates. Then a friend of his became ill. Though he became sicker and sicker, officials ignored his condition. Finally, his mother demanded that he be moved to a hospital, where he was diagnosed with terminal stomach cancer. Heavily drugged, he wasted away; nonetheless, a guard was kept in the room at all times. At the moment of dying, he reached out to touch his mother. The guard, always afraid of black men, leaped up to refasten the chains as he died.

What the brother realizes from the incident is the utter absurdity of the system that incarcerates him. No logic or moral purpose operates in the world he inhabits. Fear and raw power are the primary motivations of officials' behavior. His earlier responses of anger and open resistance merely reinforced the processes of oppression. The final brief narrative in the story initially seems to sentimentalize this insight. During one visit from his wife, they watch a leaf blowing around the prison yard. As the leaf rises, it moves closer to the wall. Others begin urging the leaf to make its escape. The brother connects this moment to learning that his wife is pregnant with a child, who, if a boy, will be named Chance Mandela. So when the leaf flies over the wall, it is read as hope for the end of imprisonment. Everyone cheers, and the speaker talks of it as a magical moment. The lesson is said to be one of faith: "Only way to save myself is to do it for me. I got to be the reason. I got to be worth saving. Can't live a life for nobody else. Nobody can live one for me" (17).

But the story does not end with this inspirational moment. To do so would undermine the naturalistic tone of the tale. The brother's completion of this last episode is more sobering: "I'm gonna tell you something I don't tell nobody when I tell about the leaf. The dumb thing blew back in here again" (17). This statement, as the ending of the story, brings back into focus the essential pessimism of "All Stories Are True." One can either grant the leaf anecdote allegorical significance, in which case it seems to suggest hopelessness (those imprisoned can never truly be free), or it can be seen as largely meaningless, in that the leaf is simply a physical object subject to natural forces. As such, what happens says nothing about human beings. In this latter case, it is an illusion that we can find meaning in anything outside ourselves.

The theme of the story is the need to live without that illusion, both to recognize harsh, threatening realities and to locate within oneself and others the resources to survive. The stories of Wade, the mother, the tree, and the brother are all Job-like tales of endurance without false hope. Not even the mother's religion offers the comfort of grand design or easy relief; rather, it enables her to deal with her troubles and to help her neighbor in his. Neither survival nor success are guaranteed or even probable.

Finally, there is the narrator of "All Stories Are True"—the one who, through listening and observing, brings together all the stories and reveals their truth. The stories would be lost and the voices silenced if he were not there to collect them. In the midst of contemporary decay and despair, he functions in the age-old way of the African griot by keeping alive the tales of the family and the community. By making even stories of meaninglessness part of the larger narrative, he grants them a meaning for new generations. By asserting that "all stories are true," he compels us to identify value and purpose within the postmodern landscape of contemporary African-American life.

"Everybody Knew Bubba Riff"

Doreatha Mbalia has argued that *All Stories Are True* represents Wideman's most complete development of the "African personality" in his fiction and, consequently, his most thoroughgoing repudiation of Western identity and values.[4] "Everybody Knew Bubba Riff" clearly challenges that assessment. As a 10-page unpunctuated, often free-association thought string, it is a stream-of-consciousness narrative in the Joycean and Faulknerian tradition. It opens with echoes of Joyce's *Finnegans Wake* and with a paraphrase of Heraclitus on the nature of time. Wideman questions this Eurocentric tradition in the sense that he shifts the Heraclitan reference from time to voice and the Joycean technique from the individual to the group. In the process, he creates a communal portrait of the title character that offers several aspects of his personality.

The method of the story allows some melding of voices, but primarily it involves extended commentaries by individual voices who knew Bubba in distinct circumstances. These voices both complement and contradict each other in the process of revealing his life and death. In addition, Wideman is clearly suggesting a jazz narrative through his use of the word *riff.* The story could be read as a series of improvisations on its subjects. In standard usage, however, *riff* refers not to improvisation but to the repeated phrase played by the ensemble behind the soloist.

The word choice indicates not difference but sameness in the pattern of voices. Thus, although the speakers have different relationships to Bubba and different life circumstances, they all either have the same view of him or believe themselves to have a truth about him that all others share. In this sense, the story reflects the title of the collection, though it does so problematically. If the voices share the same understanding, then the narrative is communal and consistent with Mbalia's reading of Wideman's work.

But in several ways, the author seems to be signifying on an Afrocentric notion as well as on a Eurocentric one. It is important to acknowledge that the various speakers share certain views about Bubba. One is that he was intensely aggressive. His mother, recalling his infancy, comments that he would bite hard on her nipple while nursing. She does not mitigate the pain, even in memory, though she does not blame him; her response, as will be seen, is part of the problem. His stepfather remembers a disrespectful young man who threatened him for attempting discipline. And a friend from their gang days talks about his bullying ways in the neighborhood. Each voice presents an antihero and shares not so much common values as a mutual understanding of Bubba as incipient criminal. The story has a number of connections with "Tommy" of *Damballah*. Here, instead of the viewpoint of the criminal, we get the perspectives of those in his life. But the wasteland imagery, including the pointlessness of the lives of young black men, is much the same. The difference is that, because multiple viewpoints are represented, there is a broader sense of why the central character became what he did and why he was destroyed.

Wideman suggests, through the thoughts of the mother and the stepfather, that a key factor in Bubba's development was the indulgence of his mother. Her passages deal only with his early childhood, which she insists on making sound happy: "my sweet Bubba how I loved that boy seem like he came out smiling like he arrived here knowing something that he him the grinningest baby you ever seen he was easy easy girl my first and the only easy one I ever had" (65). Even the biting mentioned earlier is excused: "let him nibble if he needs to nibble" (66). The mother here is in sharp contrast to Lizabeth in "Solitary," who is deeply troubled by what has happened to her son and what responsibility she might bear. Bubba's mother is sentimental and narcissistic, as are several of the characters in this story.

The stepfather is the reverse of the mother in that he sees Bubba as nothing but a problem from early childhood. He reads him as aggressive, spoiled, and in adolescence, even dangerous. Bubba grows so fast and so big that he is a financial burden in terms of shoes, clothes, and food. But the stepfather also reveals himself as abusive by recalling a confrontation: "I'ma break you in half old man don't care how much my mama need the shit you bring around here no more whipping on me you touch me or put a hand on her ever again it's rumble time mano a mano" (65). This father figure fits the classic image of the stepparent in his cruelty and in the hostility he inspires. Like the mother, he refuses to take responsibility for what the child becomes.

Part of the point of using interior monologues (including memories of dialogue) seems to be to demonstrate the lack of insight of the central characters. This is in contrast to the use of this technique in earlier stories. The characters themselves are stereotypical, and they provide little understanding of the focal figure. Primarily they offer evasions of their responsibility for Bubba's life and death. In this way, Wideman renders problematic Afrocentric notions of the centrality of family and ancestry, as well as the concept of the African personality. Not only Bubba (through others' recollections) but the others offer portraits of a self-deluding, self-serving consciousness. Although it can be argued that such portraits reveal the destructiveness of a Eurocentric individualism, they do not provide any alternative.

Another irony of the story is that the voice (or possibly voices) of outside knowledge is more perceptive about Bubba's character than are the more intimate ones. This speaker takes up most of the text. It is a voice conscious of its own desires and thus able to provide some difference from Bubba. For this speaker, the church is a place of both duty and sensuality. He remembers his adolescent desire for one of the adult women of the church, a desire that is revealed in his return for the funeral. The duty aspect was always presented to him as a difference from Bubba, who did not attend services or participate in church projects, despite his mother's requests.

This voice also provides a sense of history that otherwise is absent from the narrative. He recalls telling Bubba several times the story of Charley Rackett, a former slave. Rackett was known as the African because he spoke a "bubba dubba language" and generally refused to speak English. This refusal cost him physical punishment, which seems to have had little effect. In these qualities he appears to be a version of Orion from "Damballah." After emancipation, when Charley was very old, he still insisted on going to the fields each day, despite his inability to work. It is his toughness that the speaker and Bubba admire. Also important is the narrator's direct connection to the old man. It is a story of "my people"; in contrast, Bubba claims to have no heritage: "you said you never had no people your Mama found you out in the trash" (69). The speaker's relationship to the tale is so strong that he reports some of it as an eyewitness. The contrast is important in understanding Bubba's character. Unlike his friend, he has no sense of history or change; he believes only in the present. For him, Charley Rackett's story is an "old timey" tale, not an ongoing relationship.

Nevertheless, this speaker suggests that Bubba may be a displaced, emptied-out version of the ancestral figure. In describing Bubba's offenses in the community, which led to his murder, he refers to him as a "throwback." He carried a ball bat and used it, along with his physical size, to intimidate and rob others. He preferred direct confrontation and combat; it was, in effect, the measure of his manhood. But the culture of the streets changed, much as "Tommy" indicated earlier. Where once Bubba, the narrator, and their gang ruled, now there is no interest in glory or physical prowess:

> [D]ude making it on the street today got to have computers and beep-ers no time for cowboys and indins and gorillaing people's dope that two-bit King Kong gangster jive ain't what's happening out here today it's business business build yourself an organization man power to the people good product good distribution good vibes spread a little change around keep the boy off your back everybody gets what they want plenty to go around. (72–73)

In such a world, Bubba is not merely an anomaly; he is a disruption to the economic, criminal order. And because this new order has no respect for what came before, he can be destroyed in a cold-blooded fashion, and very few people will care. Even the speaker says that he has to "chill out" because he will go crazy if he thinks too much about the numbers of black men being killed.

Finally, then, the title of the story is deeply ironic. Not even the most thoughtful of the voices can give us much insight into Bubba. Everybody knows him in the way they know all the killed and killing black men. He is known for his violence and his "rep" on the street; he is known by the excuses offered by those who claim to have loved him. He is, in the narrative, nothing other than performance and appearance; he is the Other of those who tell of him. He is not granted interiority or subjectivity. Even the reflective friend offers little of Bubba (though much of himself) other than his actions.

In effect, Wideman uses a modernist technique to present a post-modernist character. Stream of consciousness functions here to subvert interiority. Bubba is the world's construction of the contemporary black man—a violent, posturing shell whose existence has no positive meaning. He is familiar to everyone because there is nothing to know. But at the same time, the anonymous narrator suggests an alternative. History (personal, familial, cultural), connectedness, and authentic desire can generate a self. The reader knows more of the unnamed narrator than of Bubba because the narrator speaks of himself, not narcissistically but as part of an individual life, a set of valued relationships (including one with Bubba), and an intimate link to the past. He has felt desire, made mistakes, adjusted to change, and undertaken to comprehend the world in which he must live. Unlike Bubba, this "invisible man" is the one we really know.

"Backseat"

"Backseat" returns to the concern with family and with the quest for meaning. The narrator (named John Edgar Wideman) tells stories of his relationship with his paternal grandmother and the people, places, and experiences associated with her. These include his own early sexual activities, which took place at her home. The story takes place just before and after her death. Thus the narrative makes the classic connection between love and death; however, the connection is indirect and metaphoric. John's sexual adventures are clearly separated from the stories of the grandmother and from the death theme. His adventures in effect serve as frame for the central narrative of family. Within that narrative are episodes of Martha Wideman's own intimate life as well as experiences that she and the narrator have together or separately of death, racism, and family. Continuing the theme of "All Stories Are True," the narrator gives voice to the significance of her life, even to matters about which she chose to keep silent.

The story opens with the recollection that overtly gives it its title. On a trip back home to Pittsburgh, John meets with friends, including the girl with whom he had sex many years before in the backseat of a rusting Lincoln Continental that sat in his grandmother's backyard. The memory is comic, with emphasis on the awkwardness of young bodies and the fear of discovery. The telling elides the descriptions of the car and the girl:

> Trying to hide and pretend she ain't with you. A fine ride in its day. King of the highway. It was the first year Lincoln put out the Continental, I think. Uncle Mac said when you're old enough to get a license, you can have it. Fix it up. Drive it away. I'm through with it. Just lean on back, girl. Cock your leg up out the way. (23)

A few lines later the girl is compared to a geometry compass in terms of her leg movement. The diction invites double entendre: girl as machine, car as woman. The bravado, arrogance, and power of the passage sets up a strong contrast with the central narrative that follows. And in its presentation as memory (John recalls the experience while talking to a male friend), it suggests male innocence of the realities of life for black women.

The physicality of the sexual memory is set against the wasting away of the grandmother as she dies. A large, strong woman, she has been reduced to "skin and bones," a condition that, the narrator worries, "makes my grandmother too little, too frail for the journey ahead of her" (24). Her smallness and the notion of journey leads to a memory of her taking him on the funicular when he was a small child. He recalls primarily his fascination with the lights and shapes of the city. She has aided the memory by describing the song he made up on this magical night. The episode does not relate directly to what comes either before or after. It serves to make clear the structure of "Backseat" as a collection of memories, some of which, like this one, seem complete in themselves. The links to other parts of the story are associational rather than tightly plotted. Wideman as author seeks to register the operations of human memory rather than to create a unified short story. The unity is in the subject—the grandmother—rather than in a sequence of interrelated episodes leading to a clear resolution. Moreover, the concern is not for the grandmother's life in itself but for its significance for the family and specifically for the grandson-narrator. Just as they share and mutually recall the funicular ride, so the story as a whole is a collaboration of their memories and experiences.

Thoughts about the grandmother's dying bring back memories of the first family death of John's conscious life, that of his maternal grandfather, John French. This episode, with the old man dying in the too-small bathroom of his house, has been told earlier in Wideman's fiction ("The Chinaman"), but here the emphasis is on the narrator's impressions: "It was that rush into the winter streets, a deep stillness in my mother I knew I should not violate, the questions I couldn't ask, the foolishness and fear hitting me I knew better than to act out in the ride to Finance Street . . ." (27). But more than the recollections of desire, wonder, and death that the narrator more or less links to the grandmother, there is the need to make sense of her life itself. It is a life with experiences that he cannot know. The physical distances and journeys that are a motif also include mysteries and silences that he can fill only with his speculations. This is a woman, for example, who had four husbands. The change from the first, the narrator's grandfather, to the second, the owner of the Lincoln, is handled in one sentence: "Mr. Mackinley Overton who became Uncle Mac when Grandma left Harry Wideman and moved into Overton's place above the Ricks' garage" (33). How or why this happened remains unnarrated. The conflicts and feelings involved, the consequences of the action, and the implications for the grandmother's sensual life are all left unexplored.

The last of these issues exists as a carefully evaded topic throughout the story. John parenthetically inserts into another episode a memory of surprising his grandmother one day while she was taking a bath. The bracketing is a way of simultaneously acknowledging and dismissing the significance of the moment. The episode in which it appears is one in which a neighborhood boy, ignorant of the grandmother's relationship to John, makes lewd comments about her. John makes some effort to fight over the insult, but the scene and his action are ambivalent:

> But it wasn't exactly clear if putting somebody's grandmother in the dirty dozens was as bad as putting somebody's mama there. Could be worse. Maybe. But it wasn't clear. We fought anyway, more scuffle than fight. . . . It wasn't even about who was badder, who could whip whose behind, it was about attitude. An ass whipping no matter who won, wouldn't adjust Patchhead's attitude. I should have tried anyway. He gave me an opening and I should have finished it there and then. (37)

What is significant here is the loss of the insult as the key issue. By the end, the grandmother's honor and name have been lost in the drive for male domination, and in the rules of male ritual that question whether and when a female relative's sexuality is an authorized topic for comment. The renderings of the husbands, the nakedness, and the insult all indicate the narrator's discomfort in examining the womanhood of the central character. He hints at her being an object of desire, even for himself, but then resists his thought.

He is much more comfortable discussing race and death as they apply to her. He recalls an incident from his childhood when she takes him to visit the white family for whom she works. Whereas she sees the visit as a moment of pride, he recalls primarily his discomfort and even anguish in a white environment. His five-year-old mind conjures up an angry lion, ready to destroy him, that dominates the breakfast room. This image remains with him, even years after he has forgotten other facts:

> But the experience was dreadful. I summon it up and not many details remain. No specific Rick faces. No Rick names. Just a collective, over-whelming white presence, the smells and noises of the white people responsible. Fear of scrambled eggs overcome, a thousand other fears rushing to fill the vacuum. A funny, deadly lion that somehow accom-panied me home, miniaturized but not one iota less threatening or dangerous, bounding up onto a shadowy ledge in the cave of my heart where it feigns sleep but never closes one yellow cat's-eye. (36)

The present tense of the final sentence implies the continuing dread of whiteness in the narrator's present life. And though he assigns respon-sibility for the dread to the Ricks, he also deletes any reference to sym-pathetic understanding on the part of his grandmother. At no point does she seem aware of the trauma the black child is experiencing or of its lasting effects. Again, a story in which she is directly involved becomes *his* story, and she is relegated to an ambiguous role.

Two other episodes, both of which he insists are central to under-standing her character, involve sexuality and death respectively. The first has to do with the grandmother's origins. In a conversation with the narrator a few years before her death, she reveals that she was the illegitimate child of a white man. This was never acknowledged in the small Pennsylvania town where she was born; the father never recog-nized her as his own:

> Though she was called Martha Lawson, Rutledge her real name she said. Her father a white man named Rutledge. She didn't use the word "illegitimate," but when I asked her if she meant that Rutledge was her natural father but never married her mother, she nodded and replied, Uh huh, a loud definite *uh huh* her eyes fixed directly into mine. (29)

This narrative of bastardy is not developed. Instead, the narrator chooses to expand on that "uh huh" as her commentary on history and race. It becomes a meditation on the status of white men and black women in late-nineteenth-century America. Her simple answer serves as self-affirmation in defiance of the social condition of invisibility that has been her life. It is her dismissal of her natural father and of all white men like him whose hypocrisy and immorality are responsible for much of the world's suffering.

Or at least this is the contention of the narrator, for he admits that she gives him very little information or expression of feeling: "I'm beginning to fabricate what might have been said. Devise a history I don't know. We can guess it, can't we. Crucial features, at least" (31). Since she does not offer the history directly, he reads an alternative text, her face, as memories flash through her mind:

> Yet I could read things happening in her eyes, in the corners of her mouth where age lines, incised like tribal markings, twitched. Off a screen inside her brow a third unseen eye was reading the story of her life. Pages, chapters consumed faster than a blink. Years, decades displayed on the screen, handfuls of years chewed and swallowed and savored or spit out between breaths. Her long history was being enacted again, her face betrayed the action in minute adjustments. Her chipmunk cheeks, the only place she ever got fat, trembling, flexing, bitten from inside, expressive as the skin of a lake. (31–32)

Her body again becomes a source of knowledge in the silence of her voice. The narrator must imagine the stories and the feelings; he considers himself a competent reader of her body language. But the effect is one of distance and mystery; there remains a fundamental uncertainty about the meaning of her "uh huh" and her facial expression. The narrative suggests the limits of knowledge about the past, even in its personal form. Although the story demonstrates a need to record history and memory and to seek its significance, it also expresses skepticism about our ability to do so. The best we can do is to reconstruct faithfully or invent a past that has value to us.

The final subject crucial to understanding the grandmother is the death of her son Eugene. He died in Guam a few days after World War II ended. Discussion of his death occurs at various points in the story. At one such point, the narrator does what he did with his grandmother's silence; he constructs his own meaning:

My father's dead brother Eugene, lost in one war, says this about the latest [the Gulf War]: They're crowing about winning. You watch. In a while it'll turn to Jim Crowing. Then what will those black boys think who risked their lives and lost their lives to keep a grin on the face of the man who rode Willie Horton bareback to the White House. Twelve, fourteen cops on TV beating that boy [Rodney King] with sticks long as their legs. Our young men not even home good from the war yet. What you think they be thinking when they see a black man beat to his knees by a whole posse of cracker cops. Somebody ought to tell them boys, ought to have told me, it happens every time. After every war. (28)

Part of Wideman's strategy in this story is to connect the past to the present. And he does so not merely by making personal connections but by breaking into the narrative with historical and political analysis, as he does here, and with the story of his grandmother's white father. Again, it is the narrator's interests and concerns that are primary, not those of family members. He absorbs their beings and experiences into his subjective reality; their voices and lives are not independent of his.

These relatives also serve to reflect his worldview. He seeks to explain the "iron" and "reserve" of Martha's personality by imagining her anxiety over Eugene's safety in combat. The narrator pictures her as a "crazy woman," waiting each day for the mailman to bring his letters: "Perhaps she'd exhausted every ounce of emotional energy and disciplined herself to live on what was left. Shadows and substance" (42). The end of all her worry and suffering is absurd: "weeks, months" after the war ends, she receives a telegram announcing his death, which occurred after the war was over. He imagines (she never talked about it) that the pointlessness of it all gave her a kind of "ice" that refused open emotional expression.

The end of the story is the closing frame of the narrator's first sexual experience and comes right after he describes his failure to visit his grandmother before her death. Given the discussion of her "ice," the episode of her death, with the focus on him, suggests a generational connection. He talks *about* feelings but does little to express them. Turning back to his own childhood as the conclusion reinforces the distance between generations. It also genders sexuality, for him as male innocence, and for her, with its associations with race, troubled marriage, parenthood, and death, as female suffering. Though he has known her all his life, she remains somehow "other" and mysterious, with experiences he can only guess at and impose meanings on. Although the story can be seen as a eulogy for a strong black woman, it is, at another level, the tale of the anxiety of a man who remains in the "backseat" of human understanding.

"Newborn Thrown in Trash and Dies"

"Newborn Thrown in Trash and Dies" leaves aside concern for the Homewood family and turns to the more general issue of the condition of contemporary society. The device used is the voice of a newborn girl who has been thrown down a trash chute by her mother. The title comes from a newspaper headline; Wideman chooses to give voice to one who never has the opportunity to develop a voice. The enabling assumption of the story is that instead of the clichéd flashback of our lives just before death, we in fact experience a flash-forward just after birth, which we then forget as we live our lives. Thus the baby knows the life it would have had and has something to narrate; moreover, the language she speaks can be sophisticated and even world weary. The narrative is structured according to the floors of the building, though they quickly become philosophical and even allegorical rather than literal narrative stages.

In "Floor Ten" the narrator suggests that her story is an oft-repeated one and associates this claim with the assertion that, because "they" are endlessly talking, sooner or later they are going to hit upon her particular narrative. "They" has no specific referent, but its meaning is developed through the story as the discourse of mass culture that endlessly produces trivia for a consumerist society. So much noise robs individual lives and stories of their human significance and value.

"Floor Nine" is a meditation on luck, which the narrator sees as rigged. In an inner-city project such as this one, very little money comes in from the outside world, so what is there must be recycled through gambling and acts of violence. This section serves as a commentary on the economic injustice that produces the despair of the narrator's mother. Those without opportunities for meaningful employment and economic security put their faith in chance, in con games, and in the luck that always turns out bad. Such belief is the only alternative to despair.

The "Floor of Facts" establishes some of the hard information about the narrator and her brief life. It also demonstrates Wideman's tendency to base his fiction on real events, thus blurring the line between fiction and history. All of the "facts" of the narrative are drawn from the *New York Times* article cited in this section, including the title, the names of the reporter who wrote the story and the caretaker who found the body, and details about the building. What Wideman does, then, is provide perspective on the story rather than create it. The perspective, that of the dying infant, serves to "defamiliarize," or make strange, the experience. The child notes in this section that the news story offers what is relatively "fit to print" (123). In fact, the *Times* did not follow up on the story, though the mother was charged with second-degree murder. The short story presented here builds on its reality base by inviting readers to see the victim as a person, even if one whose life was so short: "I believe facts sometimes speak for themselves but never speak for us. They are never anyone's voice and voices are what we must learn to listen to if we wish ever to be heard" (124).

The "Floor of Questions" is brief: "Why" is the only question, but it is of course the central one. If it is applied to the mother's motives, then it cannot be answered, since she has no voice in the narrative. If it concerns the brief life and death of the child, then it opens up a whole series of social issues, some of which are addressed in the remaining pages. One response the narrator offers is that her death "will serve no purpose":

> The streetlamps will pop on. Someone will be run over by an expensive car in a narrow street and the driver will hear a bump but consider it of no consequence. Junkies will leak out the side doors of this gigantic mound, nodding, buzzing, greeting their kind with hippy-dip vocalizations full of despair and irony and stylized to embrace the very best that's being sung, played and said around them. (124–25)

In other words, life goes on, and the infant's life will have made no difference. Moreover, the human lives that continue have little more value than her own. The world is a wasteland in the place where she dies.

The "Floor of Wishes" is a sentimental moment in the story, as the child realizes that she will never experience Christmas, which "seems to be the best time to be on earth, to be a child and awaken with your eyes full of dreams and expectations and believe for a while at least that all good things are possible—peace, goodwill, merriment, the raven-maned rocking horse you want to ride forever" (125–26). Christmas signifies all that childhood ought to be: wonder, belief, trust, love—precisely those things that the narrator will never have. But this desire is contextualized by the reality that what the narrator receives on her birthday is her own death, "pitched without a kiss through a maroon door" (126). Wideman suggests here the distance between even a simplified version of childhood desire, one lacking in commercialized aspects, and the utter deprivation of the lives of the unwanted.

The measure of indifference to her life has in part to do with "The Floor of Power." In rather straightforward allegory, Wideman describes "El Presidente" and his control over the building:

> Some say he owns the whole building. He believes he owns it, collects rents, treats the building and its occupants with contempt. He is a bold-faced man. Cheeks slotted nose to chin like a puppet's. Chicken lips. This floor is entirely white. A floury, cracked white some say used to gleam. El Presidente is white also. Except for the pink dome of his forehead. Once, long ago, his flesh was pink head to toe. Then he painted himself white to match the white floor of power. (126)

El Presidente's job is to maintain the status quo, to keep the building from ever improving. El Presidente represents not a single individual but the structure that reinforces the hopelessness of those like the narrator's mother. "Whiteness" indicates an institutionalized racism, which, though absurd, continues to signify power and perpetuate the suffering of those who must live in the "building."

But despair also resides in more intimate space, on "The Floor of Love." Here the narrator fantasizes an idealized family life, with good food and caring, attentive parents. The narrative shifts abruptly and without preparation into a more brutal scenario. Here the father sexually abuses the daughter, and she cooperates because she has learned that her mother will beat her if she tells. Cooperation is a way of getting it over with sooner. Just as in the political realm, so here there is no alternative to suffering; in fact, it may be worse in that the pain is generalized under El Presidente but personal with the parents. The daughter needs a fantasy of love to live in her home, but in fact the same stark contrast exists between desire and reality. Even if the narrator had lived, we are thus led to understand, she would have suffered on every "floor" of her experience.

The concluding section, "The Floor That Stands for All the Other Floors Missed or Still to Come," tells the story of the narrator's brother Tommy, killed accidentally in a drive-by shooting. While everyone mourns, his brother and fellow gang members plot revenge, thus perpetuating the cycle of violence. What the narrator notes is that Tommy is beginning to remember her and join her in the death journey. Another child becomes part of the garbage society gets rid of. In a link to earlier tales, Tommy is the name Wideman gives to the imprisoned brother in the *Damballah* stories; he clearly expands outward the notion of lost and wasted children.

The last lines of the story indicate its larger purpose: "Tommy is beginning to remember me. To join me where I am falling unseen through your veins and arteries down down to where the heart stops, the square opening through which the trash passes to the compactor" (128). The shift to imagery of the body and to second-person reference forces on the reader an engagement with the narrative voice and thus some responsibility for the events of the story. All of us destroy children if we allow our hearts to "stop," as long as we consider them "trash" to be disposed of. In this context, Wideman is commenting on the decision of the *Times* not to follow the story; such families as the one in "Newborn," both parents and children, are disposable.

"Signs"

"Signs," the final story to be discussed here, is also in some ways the most complex. The others consistently validate the voices of the texts and affirm the title of the collection. No matter how difficult it is to locate truth, the stories in some way embody it. The focal character of "Signs" is different in that she ultimately undercuts the truth value of her tale through her confession of unreliability; in this very act, however, she raises doubts about her revised "truth."

The story seems a relatively straightforward moral narrative about racism. A young black woman in graduate school begins to experience literal signs of race antagonism: epithets and veiled threats in notes at her office and dormitory are clearly directed at her. Because she is the first college-educated member of her family and is insecure about her achievement, even before the signs, she experiences considerable stress in her life. This sometimes leads to bizarre thought processes, even while in the midst of a discussion of Milton with a student:

> Gooey stuff from her exploded head sticks to the ceiling. Viscous, elongated drops plop down onto the desk. Drip-drop. Drippity drop. Out the windows bells and children playing the waddle of web-footed birds walking across water. I know it's not easy Bobby Baby [the student].

See these wounds in my palms. If I unbuttoned this desk from my waist and let it float down around my slim ankles and lifted my naked foot for you to inspect you'd find a ten-penny nail hole bored through my instep. (79)

This thought sequence occurs while she is explaining very formally some key themes in *Paradise Lost*. The contrast of discourses, as well as the shift from limited third-person to first-person voice, strengthens the disorienting effects of the story.

Blended into this pattern are memories of home, of her dead mother and the two great-aunts who raised her. In fact, she repeatedly suggests a tension between the worlds of home and education that is fundamental to her identity. Additionally, she fantasizes a lover, who is never made specific but who is associated with home, even though her aunts trained her to "[leave] that nasty snake alone" (76). Thus we are presented with a central character who is conflicted in her allegiance, insecure about her abilities, and under stress to perform.

The signs intrude into this environment. The first—a "Whites Only" sign posted on the door of the dormitory restroom—she takes as a joke in poor taste. The posting takes place, after all, "on an integrated campus in the post-emancipation, post-riots, post-civil rights, post-equal opportunity, post-modern last decade of the twentieth century" (80). At the same time, she feels a combination of shame and anger as she tears the cardboard into tiny pieces and throws it into the trash. She speculates that it may have been done by one of the black men in the same graduate program, though the motives are obscure. Following this experience a note is slipped under her door, "*Nig bitch go home*" (83), and then a large "KKK" is chalked on the door. As she washes off the chalk, she wonders why the other women on the floor have not commented: "Why hadn't one of them come forward" (83).

After three weeks of additional signs, she makes an appointment with the dean, the man who recruited her to the university. What she receives from him, however, is not sympathy but hypocrisy. Although he speaks the appropriate words, he is, from her perspective, primarily concerned with his own reputation and that of the institution. A similar pattern occurs when she takes her complaints to a group of black students. Here she finds a great deal of posturing and political argument but very little attention to her situation or emotions. They dispute tactics and strategies and insult each other, but nothing comes of the effort.

In the narrator's experiences with the dean and the black students, Wideman seems to be suggesting priority of ideology and self-aggrandizement over the realities of human suffering. The similarities are apparent in masculine assertiveness, in reliance on jargon, and in the effective discounting of the female voice. Though the discourses are different, the underlying motivations and values are the same. The dean and the students are oriented toward power, not toward actual need. In this, they seem little different from the perpetrator of the signs.

Her response to a speaker from South Africa gets at the central issue for her. When he is asked about the practice of "necklacing" (that is, hanging burning tires around the necks of suspected informers), he answers by explaining the importance of trust in an oppressive environment. The narrator turns the thought inward:

> Does she inform on herself. Does a traitor lurk in her heart passing on her secrets to the authorities. The fear of one shuts down trust. If she cannot trust herself, is she fatally divided. Which voice the traitor—the one keeping her here at school or the one calling her home. What's being betrayed—her wish to be a person the signs can't turn around, or is the person holding on, fighting for a place in this wilderness betraying the one who knows good and well being here is wrong. (92)

The story's conclusion is an apparent confession that she in fact produced the signs herself. She acknowledges to the reader that she had access to all the necessary materials. The admission comes just after she learns of the deaths of her two aunts in an automobile accident. Her motive is unclear even to herself, though she tells the dean that it was stress and expresses the belief that it will not happen again. The motive seems clearer in the passage cited above, in which she puzzles over self-betrayal and the two versions of her identity. Is the one who moves out into the larger world, and thus engages in defiance of racism and discrimination, the hero of her self-narrative? Or is it the one connected to home, who knows that the world does not change and that engaging it is in some sense becoming "white"? In terms of this conflict, the "home" self seeks to guarantee the failure of the "worldly" self by generating signs that are unmistakable.

This reading implies the self-dividing and self-defeating effects of racism on the black psyche. American racial realities produce a predisposition to assuming that the world remains a dangerous place for

African Americans, a place to be avoided to the extent possible. The ambiguity of the ending—"But how could she have spoken to herself on the phone" (94)—indicates that the "facts" of the case are less important than the narrator's mental state. Given a world in which race is a fact of everyday life and racism continues to be part of the social structure, it does not really matter whether the signs are bad jokes, racial threats, or self-destructive gestures. Whatever the motive or source, they are the product of an ongoing social order that seeks the narrator's failure. Even if the signs are self-generated, they are the product of generations of real fear and social insecurity that one individual may not be able to overcome. So although this may be a tale of paranoia or divided personality, Wideman suggests that the real disorder—racism—remains virulent, a "fever" even, in society. In this sense, then, even a story in which the truth cannot be easily discerned remains a truthful tale.

As "Signs" and the other stories from this collection suggest, Wideman is not hopeful about contemporary American society. These narratives challenge the social and political claims that we have reached a point at which race and other social "problems" are not factors in individual achievement. He speaks for and as those whose voices have been denied or suppressed, and in the process he challenges what might be called the master narrative of American freedom and individualism. By placing in the foreground the ideological character of the nation's stories, he places himself among the postmodernists. He operates within the paradox that if "all stories are true," then the very meaning of truth is problematic. But his postmodernism grows out of a deep commitment to the past and to traditional cultural values. Ancestors in this as well as the earlier books are crucial to a sense of self. It is those without such connections, as in "Newborn," or those who are losing connection, as in "Signs," who are the lost and victimized. In a world of prisoners, unwanted children, and exploited women, the harshness of reality cannot be ignored. To pretend either that they do not exist or that there are easy solutions to the situations they represent is both foolish and cruelly irresponsible. One way to make them visible in a world that does not want to see is to tell their stories, even if only by imagining them. Ironically, telling tales of alienation, violence, and death makes possible an affirmation of their lives by giving them a humanity too often denied them in life. In this sense, Wideman might be called a postmodern moralist in that he demands attention to the moral implications of life in a world lacking a moral sensibility.

Notes to Part 1

1. *The Stories of John Edgar Wideman* (New York: Pantheon Books, 1992), 272. All further references to Wideman's stories are taken from this collection and cited in the text.

2. See Jacques Lacan, *Ecrits: A Selection,* trans. Alan Sheridan (New York: W. W. Norton, 1977), 67.

3. See Henry Louis Gates, *The Signifying Monkey: A Theory of Afro-American Literary Criticism* (New York: Oxford University Press, 1988), 44–88, on the idea of signifying in African-American literature.

4. Doreatha Drummond Mbalia, *John Edgar Wideman: Reclaiming the African Personality* (Selinsgrove, Penn.: Susquehanna University Press, 1995), 113.

Part 2

THE WRITER

Introduction

The interviews with Wideman, as might be expected, have focused largely on the relationship between his life and his writing. Given the extent to which he has brought family history into his narratives, especially his short fiction, the interviewers have focused on that process. At the same time, that choice has implications for how Wideman's work is to be read. Attention to African-American life has the potential to limit the audience, if the assumption is made that that subject is provincial. Wilfred Samuels specifically asks about this aspect of the work and draws out Wideman's view that particularity, not generality, is the way to present the human experience most effectively. Similarly, the author expresses concern about the role of mainstream critics in commenting on black writing. He sees them as often narrow in their understanding and as committed to an ideological position. Thus the Samuels interview serves to define Wideman's attitudes toward his own work and his audience at the beginning of his short-story writing career.

Charles Rowell, in his 1990 interview, complements Samuels by asking much more about Wideman's career development and his relationships with literary movements, such as the black arts movement of the 1960s. This leads to a discussion of the function of the writer and whether the African-American artist has a special role in literature. Because the interview took place a short time after the publication of *Fever,* Rowell raises questions about both the structure of that collection and its use of public, as opposed to private, history. In the conversation, which also involves a comparison of that work with *Damballah,* they discuss Wideman's own role as a critic of black writing and why he considers that role an important one.

Jessica Lustig returns to the notions of place and family in her 1992 *African American Review* interview. The emphasis in this case is on Homewood as a fictional construct rather than a place with biographical connections. This perspective offers a view of what might be called Wideman's theory of fiction in that it concerns the way he consciously transforms experience into literature. Much more apparent here than in the earlier interviews is what might be called an Africanist point of view. He sees the Homewood of his writing as reflecting survivals of an African sensibility. Finally, he discusses why Homewood is so central to his writing, despite his experiences in other places.

These interviews reveal a writer who has thought a great deal about his craft and about his relationship to audience, material, and profession. Wideman reveals a considerable social awareness but maintains a belief that his artistry is his primary responsibility.

Going Home: A Conversation with John Edgar Wideman

WIDEMAN: According to the family history, my great-great-great-grandmother was one of the first people to settle in Homewood.

SAMUELS: Does she become the Sybela in your short stories?

WIDEMAN: Yes. Sybela is based on that female ancestor. My Aunt May, who lives in Pittsburgh, is the only family member left who actually saw Sybela. The way I spell it in the stories is "Sybela." But I have never seen it written; I have only heard people say her name. If two relatives are sitting around, one will say "Sybela" and the other will say "Sivela." So who knows?

SAMUELS: The one remaining relative, May, did you say?

WIDEMAN: Yes, May.

SAMUELS: May. Again, there is a character like her in your short stories. And the one thing that struck me about her is that she is a kind of *griot*, in the African sense: she is the story teller, the family historian who knows the lore of the family. Did you have this in mind when you created that character and placed her in the stories (and novel), or is May based on your family member?

WIDEMAN: There is always the reciprocity between fictional and real characters, but certainly the actual May came first and there are all sorts of close linkages between the actual Aunt May and the Aunt May in the stories. But the Aunt May in the stories is very definitely based on a particular human being I've known all my life.

SAMUELS: How old is she now?

WIDEMAN: May is about seventy-five now. When she saw Sybela Owens, Aunt May was a tiny girl, and Sybela Owens, a very old woman. But they did meet. There is another woman in Homewood who remembers Sybela. This woman is not a member of the family, but she is very close to us. Her name is Elizabeth Lewis, and she, also, has memories of Sybela Owens. She said that Sybela Owens always wore a black cape.

SAMUELS: Is that right?

Wilfred D. Samuels, "Going Home: A Conversation with John Edgar Wideman," *Callaloo* 6.1 (February 1983): 40–59. ©1983. The Johns Hopkins University Press.

WIDEMAN: Interestingly enough, my grandfather, Harry Wideman, who migrated to Pittsburgh from South Carolina when he was a young man, actually climbed Bruston Hill and did some work for Sybela Owens. The incident occurred long before my father was born, long before my mother was born. Harry Wideman climbed up the hill and saw Sybela.

SAMUELS: So Homewood and Bruston Hill are real, physical places, not just a fictional community that you have created for your work?

WIDEMAN: Oh, no. Homewood is very real. As I said, the family history coincides with the history of the actual community. Aunt May claims that the first tree was chopped down by her great-grandfather, Charles Owens. When May was going to public school, there was a day set aside, a holiday, for celebrating the beginning of Homewood. May and her sisters would get mad because, in the story she was told in school, a man she'd never heard of was credited with founding the community by chopping down a tree. May knew better. She knew that it was Charley Owens who cut down the first tree.

SAMUELS: And Charley was Sybela's husband.

WIDEMAN: Yes. Sybela's husband, the father of her children, anyway. He was white, but he was May's relative. . . .

SAMUELS: As a critic, I would say that, from reading your last two works and from reading your earlier works, I find what could be called a "turning point": you've gone from a novel that is, in a way, raceless to one that speaks to and celebrates a particular experience. But what you are saying is that this doesn't mean that the experience becomes limited, that it is less meaningful to the human experience.

WIDEMAN: I don't have any problems with the argument that says the emphasis of my fiction has changed, that there is a more explicit concern with Afro-American life. I am not interested in investigating family and community in a generalized, universal context. My subject is a black family, a black family in America, in a particular city. On the other hand, if you're lucky and writing well, the more specific you become, the more you root what you are doing in a particular environment, the more general resonance it has. If you capture absolutely what happened to you, then other people read it and say, "Yes, I recognize myself in that," no matter what their backgrounds are. . . . I hope that is what is happening in my last two books. I hope by examining the particularity of my past that I am making it exist on its own terms—but, that at the same time, giving it a greater accessibility. . . .

SAMUELS: That is a very good point because, if I may just enter a comment here, it seems to me that the introduction to *Damballah* calls to attention a particular audience. Did you intend for that to be the case?

WIDEMAN: Oh, I wanted to get everybody's ear, but if you've read T. S. Eliot, James Joyce, or William Faulkner, you aren't excluded from *Damballah*. But those are not the only "keys to the kingdom." If you have grown up black, you also have some "keys" to what this book has to offer. Ideally, I had in mind a book that people familiar with America, with the technique and history of the novel—a book that the audience could appreciate and applaud and relate to the great traditions, if there are such things. But at the same time a book my brother, sister, aunts, uncles, cousins, mother and father could read. And in my mind it became quite clear that to do a book like that would not be writing down to a black audience, because my people have had the full range of human experience. Their feelings, thoughts, intelligence—all have been tested and been refined—so it wasn't a question of writing down to a less educated set of readers but rather to expand my own frames of reference. And my ambition still is to write as well as anybody has ever written. I am sure now that for a long time I didn't know what really counted—what would really count as legitimate subject matter, legitimate language, for such an enterprise. To write the very best, didn't you have to cheat a little, didn't you have to "transcend blackness"? Didn't you have to ground yourself in an experience that was outside . . . Homewood? Didn't you have to show you were part of a larger world? Didn't you have to show continually your credentials with allusions to the "great writers"—the "great traditions"? . . .

The first story in *Damballah* is about transformation of consciousness, about passing on experience from generation to generation, about the mysterious way such sharing takes place. The old woman in the "Chinaman Story" sees a Chinaman. In one scene the Chinaman is imaginary, yet she knows he is going to get her. And that story is almost literal. It happened to my grandmother. She had a stroke but hung on for many, many years. She began to believe she was being attacked by an evil spirit. She started muttering a word, and my uncle figured out it was "Chinaman." A little while after that, they took her to the hospital. My mother met a young Asian woman in the hospital. The young woman would sit in the lounge talking with my people because her father, like my grandmother, was bedridden in one of the hospital rooms. Her father got well, and on the way out of the hospital, she

decided to stop to say goodbye to my folks who were in with my grandmother. The Asian woman took her little Chinese father into the room
to peek at my grandmother who was sleeping. She never woke up again.
She had a premonition that a Chinaman would come to her. And he did.

SAMUELS: So what would you tell critics who might say, as is often said
about Toni Morrison, that the more you immerse yourself in the black
experience the more strains of mysticism and magic appear? For example the title of your collection of short stories might lead someone to
believe that you are bringing to your work more black or Afro-American
folklore or culture, and again, might lead him to argue that there is evidence of a kind of "turning point" in your recent work. For example, I
am not certain whether or not critics will be able to continue to make
references to your direct or indirect influences—say an Eliot or a
Joyce—because your works speak to unique aspects and elements of
Afro-American culture, specifically its folk culture.

WIDEMAN: Oh, yes. But see, the terrible thing is that as writer or critic
we are forced into these kinds of choices, and we are forced into them
because there are values attached. You can say that "Wideman is a good
writer; he uses Afro-American folklore, he knows this, that, or the other
thing about his heritage and culture." You can make that argument, and
show it in the work, and pat me on the back, but that doesn't get me out
of the ghetto. It should, but it doesn't. If I do all that, I mean that is
enough, but there is always an implied, invidious comparison: "OK,
Wideman does fine with Afro-American stuff, but on the other hand the
real writers are doing so and so. . . ." To protect ourselves as critics and
artists, we are forced to jump back and forth, measure ourselves against
an imaginary mainstream, define what we are doing in somebody else's
terms. It's almost like making excuses. It is a terrible bind.

SAMUELS: It is unfortunate, but what you've said is true. I think,
though, that what I find most pleasing when I look at your work, when I
look at Toni Morrison's work and at James Baldwin's work, is a beautiful
validation of the Afro-American experience as a vehicle for understanding what is called "the human experience." For me that is enough. I don't
need the comparisons. Why can't the blues be recognized as an art form
that speaks about alienation? Why can't the blues be accepted as a viable
and valuable vehicle for understanding the "human experience"?

WIDEMAN: Yes, I agree, but we don't have to convince each other. The
historical problem is there and how you solve it creates a sort of "out the
frying pan into the fire." There is an Afro-American tradition. There are
Afro-American writers working right now; it makes sense to talk about

them as a group, or about certain ways that their work relates. It is natural; it is enlightening; it is intelligent to do it that way, but, at the same time, to do that perpetuates the "bad side" of the whole notion of looking at things in black and white ways. You almost can't have one without the other. You see it in academia. You have someone get up to argue. If things were perfect, American literature would include writings by Baldwin. That sort of sounds good, but it is also bullshit, too, because the individual strains in the tradition are really what the tradition is. Culture is a house of cards. The parts are more tangible than the whole. A house of cards is dependent on the relationships among the cards. Its existence depends on the individual cards. The sort of shape and form that you arrive at when you pile the cards together is interesting, per se, and you can talk about it; you can analyze it; you can say this, that, and the other, but if you pull one of those cards out, the whole thing collapses. The parts are bigger than the whole. So, I like that metaphor to talk about culture, particularly American culture. . . .

I made some pretty prodigious economic leaps in my lifetime, so I have had the opportunity to observe many different kinds of people. Starting in a place like Homewood, and then going to Philadelphia to an Ivy League school, and then going abroad and studying at Oxford, and winding up in academia. Like those of many other black people, my experiences encapsulate what often took generations of living. Imagine an immigrant family at the turn of the century. The father is a tailor; he does this and then he has kids, and they get to school and maybe they become businessmen of some sort, and maybe their kids get to school and to professional school. So, literally, in the classic American pattern it takes generations. But it happened to me in a lifetime. I was the first in my family—my extended family—to go to college. I've had a chance to observe lots of people and because the world was moving so fast around me, I was really thrown on my wits a lot. I was both participating but was also forced to take the posture of an observer because I didn't know what the hell was going on. It was best to keep quiet and sort of check it out before I exposed my game. The insider/outsider nature of my experience made me a listener. I have always listened to people and watched them closely and carefully. That habit is something I can fall back on as a novelist. Yet one of my biggest regrets is that moving fast caused me to miss so much. In the writing that I have been doing for the last three or four years, I have been trying to recover some of that lost experience, to re-educate myself about some of the things I missed because the world was moving so fast. Now, I have returned to Homewood and have sort of settled in. I am trying to listen again. Fortunately, my people are being kind, compassionate, patient. They give me the benefit of the doubt. In spite of Thomas Wolfe, I can go home again; I listen again, I can learn again the things I heard and saw as a child and young man. There is a basic conservatism in any folk life. There are little sayings and phrases that I read in the WPA narratives from the thirties or in slave narratives. I'd heard them before in my living room. "Stomp down ugly." When I found that phrase in a slave narrative, I cracked up because I had been hearing that my whole life. Afro-American culture is conservative, and it does give you a chance to go back, and I have had that chance. Reading writers like Albert Murray, Leon Forrest, and of course Zora Hurston and Ellison and Richard Wright, I was reminded of things I had forgotten; books were also a way of returning.

SAMUELS: Let me ask you something about critics. How important are they to your work? Do you listen to what they have to say? Do you respond in any way to what they have to say about your work? Just how important are critics to you as a writer?

WIDEMAN: I have lots of answers to that question. Critics are extremely important if you want your stuff to be read, because they are a vehicle by which you are presented to the public. But I think very often critics frustrate this ideal function. I think that a lot of times, because of ego, because of their own limitations, they stand in the way of the work. That is frustrating, and I get furious. It's a very unfair competition because there is no real forum in which authors can answer critics' charges. If you said *Hiding Place* is a book about a guy who obviously hated his mother and wanted to destroy her by putting her up on a hill (he is afraid of women and such and such)—if you said that in an article, what could I do? Number one, anybody who reads that, the damage is done. You have gotten your word in, no matter how wrong. If a person has not read the book, then he will just assume you've reported the facts. A lot of people treat reviews that way, and it is not proper. There isn't an institutionalized way for me to answer you except to bitch at somebody in a letter to the editor, even if it is published. So it's a very one-sided kind of dialogue. That's a pain in the ass. I have had good reviews; some have been perceptive reviews. My things have gotten around to major publications, so I don't have any particular gripes. Personally, I have been treated pretty well. But as I said before, the whole vexed relationship of black literature to the mainstream, the inability of critics to treat black literature as technique, as art, the tendency of critics to use black literature as a way of trying to put forward certain ideological concerns and points of view—that has been a disaster for all black writers.

SAMUELS: That still remains true today?

WIDEMAN: Sure.

SAMUELS: In spite of the fact there are such writers of quality work as yourself, Toni Morrison, Toni Bambara, and others. I think that the Afro-American literary tradition is today in very healthy, stable shape. The quality of the works, the caliber of the writers, have never been better.

WIDEMAN: I hope that's true, and I'd probably tend to agree with you. The trouble is (and it's always been the case), who is Afro-American writing getting to; who are the people we can trust to preserve it? I know there are some good spirits out there, black and white, who really appreciate black writing for what it is worth. But the only way literature survives is through readers—because it has readers, because it has informed readers, because it has readers who love it and won't let it die. How much of our stuff is getting to black readers? Getting to the people? I know my black readership is minimal. I wish somebody would try to market black literature the way records have been marketed in the black community. Our people have always been willing to spend money for enjoyment, for entertainment, and that entertainment dollar is out there. Even when people are broke. If you could get the books in the same places that other consumer goods are, maybe the books can compete. That would make me very happy. That is why I wrote the way I did in the last two books and published them in paperbacks. I'm hoping that maybe someday one of these books will be accessible to a wide black audience. Books should be a part of the Afro-American Inheritance, as much as the music, as much as the oral culture. Books could provide ideas for raising consciousness, raising self-esteem, different models for how to live. Preservation of the past. But are good books available in most black communities? The idea that books contain the wisdom of the people, the creativity of the people, has to get back to the community. That's your job.

An Interview with John Edgar Wideman

ROWELL: John, what brought you to writing and publishing creative texts? When you were a student at the University of Pennsylvania, you were captain of the basketball team. Then later you became a Rhodes scholar at Oxford University. How did you resist becoming a professional basketball player? In other words, what made you take the risk of becoming a creative writer?

WIDEMAN: Well, for me, I guess, it wasn't really a risk. Writing was something I had done as long as I could remember—and I simply wanted to try it seriously, full-time. I was very obviously young and ignorant, and I thought if you wanted to do things and if they were important to you that you could do them. And so I had that kind of optimism and, I guess, in a way arrogance. But storytelling and writing have been a part of my life forever, and I have enjoyed them for a long time.

This goes back, Charles, to when I was in grade school in Homewood in Pittsburgh. There was no auditorium in the grade school that I went to, which, by the way, was the same one that my mother attended in the 1920s—the same building, same location, obviously, and probably the same pencils and paper, I think. But this school had no auditorium, and so any time there was an assembly people simply sat on the steps in the central hallway, and I found myself, on more than one occasion, being called out by teachers to talk to the entire school when we had an assembly, when we had a program. Also, during homeroom I would get a chance to get up and tell stories, and that was my thing. I guess I was pretty good at it, because I could hold people's attention. I was fascinated by that. Even as a kid I recognized this as power and attention— the attention that I could get, the sense of control that I could have for a few moments, and just the whole fun of spinning out a story and making something up and, as I was making it up, engaging other people. So storytelling was a very satisfactory, personal kind of experience for me, going way back.

Charles H. Rowell, "An Interview with John Edgar Wideman," *Callaloo* 13.1 (Winter 1990): 47–60. ©1990. The Johns Hopkins University Press.

And then there were great storytellers in my family, and family gatherings—picnics and weddings, church socials, funerals, wakes—were occasions for other people to exercise their storytelling abilities and talents. So I had around me a kind of world, a creative world, an imaginative world, which I could draw from and which I very much wanted to participate in.

Let me bring it a little closer to the time we're talking about. By the time I had graduated from college and had gone to graduate school, I was thoroughly interested in the romantic notion of being a writer. What power the writer could have—and now I'm talking about the literate tradition—the sense of the writer as adventurer, the writer as explorer. That part of it was something that appealed to me greatly.

ROWELL: Well, how do you move from the orality of the past—that is to say, storytelling—to the writing of stories? How does one make that transition? What in your studies at the University of Pennsylvania or Oxford University, or in your private reading, helped you to make the transition from the oral to the written?

WIDEMAN: The written had been there from the beginning. I was very lucky in school. I went to school at a time when there were teachers who encouraged writing. We were required to write, and our writing was corrected, critiqued. So writing was very natural for me. I learned to do it early and, again, I enjoyed it. I also had little stories and poems published at an early age, and this wasn't because I was particularly precocious or had any sort of unusual ability, but because I did it, I worked at it, and I was in a circumstance where people responded and reinforced that kind of activity. In that sense I was quite lucky. The reading part is again something I came to early. I loved to read. I read all the books I could get my hands on. That was a way I spent an awful lot of my time.

I was very active; I played sports. But then there were times when the sports weren't available to me. When I was about 12 years old, we moved from Homewood, which was essentially a black community in Pittsburgh, to another community that was predominantly white, middle class and upper-middle class. That meant that the very lively world of the playground, which was part of my life in Homewood, had really more or less dried up. So I had a lot of time on my hands, and I couldn't always find games. And reading became something I really enjoyed. That literate world was there from adolescence and continued to be there.

Now I think that the kind of experience, the kind of movement into writing that you asked me about, I can identify clearly the moment that it happened. It was after reading, reading, reading lots of books. I guess

I was about 16, 17, 18 years old, somewhere in there, the end of high school, early college. I began to feel that this book writing wasn't that complicated, and I had that feeling because a lot of what I read was trash. I mean I read Westerns, I read adolescence fantasy stories, I read the Tarzan and sci-fi stories of Edgar Rice Burroughs, things that were heavy on adventure and unusual characters. I began to see the formulas, I began to see how these things worked, what the parts were. And it was pretty easy for me to think at that time, "Well, hell, I can do that too." So I guess I learned to read between the lines and began to become fascinated with how things were made. And I thought I could do it. From that point on, I guess I wrote more and more, but certainly not on the scale of a novel. Yet I had just had a feeling that I possessed the requisite abilities to write a book.

ROWELL: My next question relates, in part, to the previous one on the Black Arts Movement, but its focus is what I continue to witness as the audience's demand of or prescription for black writers in the United States. How do you respond—or do you respond at all—to readers, especially black readers in the United States, frequently demanding "critical realism" from black writers? That is to say, readers so frequently desire to have the black writer engage, socially and politically, his or her own fiction. How do you respond to such a demand?

WIDEMAN: I don't respond well to anybody who tells me what to do. Whether it's in sports or dress, and certainly not in something as personal and intimate as literature. I listen and I try to make sense of criticism, but I listen much better when I'm not commanded to do something, when I don't feel pushed and shoved. So the bullyish tone and one-dimensional demands that characterized certain critics during the sixties, if anything, made me more sure that as a writer I was responsible to something other than somebody else's ideas of what I should write and how I should write. Especially since I was working very hard to escape the strictures, to break out of the mould imposed by my "classic," Europeanized education. I didn't want to be J. Alfred Prufrock, I didn't want to be Hemingway anymore, I wanted to strike out on my own. And so I wasn't looking for anybody to give me another set of parameters or another path that I had to follow or another load or burden or harness on my back. It was important that I exercise independence and find my own voice, my own prerogative, at this time.

ROWELL: I'm fascinated by your expression "intimate as literature." Will you talk about that? How is literature "intimate"? I love that phrase, "intimate as literature."

WIDEMAN: Writing for me is an expressive activity, so it's as intimate as my handwriting, or the way I dance, or the way I play basketball. And when I do those things they're not simply instrumental; that is, when I write I'm not only writing to give a message; when I play basketball I'm not doing it simply to score points or to win. But in all those activities—and I think this is true of Afro-American art in general—there are ways of being who I am, and so I need to find the space to express what I am, who I am. Writing for me is a way of opening up, a way of sharing, a way of making sense of the world, and writing's very appeal is that it gives me a kind of hands-on way of coping with the very difficult business of living a life. What could be more intimate than that, what has more significance than that? Writing is like breathing, it's like singing, it takes the whole body and mind and experience. It's also anarchistic. I like to write because it allows me to do things my way, to say them my way. So what if everybody else's way is different.

ROWELL: I want to go back to a question I asked earlier about critics' and general readers' demands on black writers. The case of Irving Howe on Richard Wright is one we all know about. Ralph Ellison and James Baldwin responded—each in his own way—to Howe. Some years later Albert Murray responded to James Baldwin in *The Omni-Americans*. Do you think this dialogue, or this discourse, is unfinished? Is the black writer now free to proceed to write? I admit, of course, the way I raise the question loads the case. You can tell where I come from aesthetically.

WIDEMAN: Number one, Charles, I'm having a hard time hearing you, but for me one of the most important functions for writing—Afro-American writing, Eskimo writing, whatever—is identical with one of the most important functions of any art, and that is to be a medium of expression, a free medium of expression, a way that people can say what they want to say, do what they want to do, play in a way that they want to play. Art should be something that in many senses goes against the grain of the culture. That's one of its values, disruptive as well as integrative. It's the place where there's craziness, where there's unpredictability, where there is freedom of expression. Art should always be something that to some degree shocks and changes people and worries people and contradicts what the king says. Achebe makes the point that the writer or the artist is always the enemy of the king. Writing, art, is subversion, it turns the world on its head, it makes up things. That's its power, that's its joy. Play, illusion. Any constraints on that, any kind of rules or any allegiances that are externally imposed, have to be looked at by the artist with a lot of suspicion, a lot of skepticism. And that's the point of view where I come from. Which is not to say that an artist cannot be socially responsible, but I think the issue here is that the notion of social responsibility is really quite a wide one. The policing of that responsibility will be done or should be done by the audience. If you are on an ego trip, if you are too deeply involved in some kind of idiosyncratic masturbatory activity, well, people will eventually peek your whole card and not care about what you do. Or critics will come down on your case, etc., etc., but we can't police the activity before things are done, we can't direct art, we can't tell people what to write about, we can't ask people to follow rules. Rules are the anathema as well as the bones of art.

ROWELL: I was going to ask you a question about the use of one's private life in one's own creative writing. I know that one's private life is often important to contemporary poetry. Is it important to the contemporary fiction writer? More specifically, is your private life, your family history, important to you as a fiction writer? How does the fiction writer transform that private life in his or her texts?

WIDEMAN: Well, my work itself is the answer to the question because I write out of who I am, and my identity and my writing identity, my life as transposed into the art that I practice, are becoming more and more of a piece. I don't make distinctions, I think that's one satisfying development; I don't make distinctions in a way that I once did. I don't think of myself as writer only when I'm sitting down in the morning at my desk in my study, scratching on a piece of paper. I use my imagination, I use what I do when I write all the time, and I feel that anything that happens to me is fair game. And more and more the subjects of the fiction are this strange interpenetration of the imagined life and the actual life and the inextricability of the two. That's what my career, if such a word is appropriate, is all about. Finding a means to live in a world and finding that art is a crucial tool for negotiating that life. This cuts in a lot of different directions; I write about the most intimate, the most personal events in my life, but the fun or the privilege of the artist is that through transformation, through the use of a medium, like language, everything becomes coded, and the reader, no matter how astute or how familiar with the writer or the writer's life, can't really decode the real life from the fictional life. So that although I tell all, I can tell it the way I want to tell it. Which doesn't exactly make the private public, because I am the one who's filtering it, I am the one controlling what goes forth. I may have a problem about something, about sleep for instance, but I can transform it into something else, a story about waking, a problem about being awake, and no one would never know what I was dealing with. Fiction/facts are what the artist creates. Good writing is always about things that are important to you, things that are scary to you, things that eat you up. But the writing is a way of not allowing those things to destroy you.

ROWELL: You've commented on your use of private history in the writing of *Fever* [1989], a collection of stories. In the title story of that collection and in your forthcoming novel [1990] on the Philadelphia Fire, you introduce us to "public history" as one of your sources. What does this mean for you as a writer? Is this another shift or stage in your writing career?

WIDEMAN: It's not exactly new because I took a lynching and made a story about that. And it wasn't based on a specific lynching, but at the beginning of the book there is a litany of actual lynchings and atrocities committed against black people. But there is a difference. I think that certain public events occur and they have lots of significance, they are very important, they define powerful currents, they are events we shouldn't ignore, that we shouldn't forget, that we should try to make sense of. But at the same time because of the speed of the media and because of the activity that goes around us all the time, the accelerated push of contemporary life, we miss these events. Then there is also the very conscious censorship and infantilization and lying and distortion the media perpetrates. And there's the political reality of the social environment that we live in, where an individual life counts for less and less. We are being pushed into a communal anthill, living willy-nilly whether we like it or not. Blackness is being attacked not simply in the old ways because of difference, difference *vis-à-vis* whiteness, but just because it's different. There's no time for somebody who asks too many questions. No time for people who want to bring up the past, and reconsider the past. There's no time for people whose lives present a different agenda than the agenda that is central—the majority agenda. And so I'm looking at this kind of situation and I see things happening and I see them getting buried. *Fever* was based on an actual occurrence of yellow fever in Philadelphia, Pennsylvania, in the 1790s. Like Antonin Artaud, I think that societies, in some metaphysical sense, create the diseases they need and that those diseases are metaphors for the basic problems of those societies. It's no coincidence that the yellow fever epidemic, described by many at the time as the end of the world, was allegedly brought to the Americas by slaves from the West Indies. We need to stop the wheel and look at things again, try to understand what they mean.

ROWELL: You have referred to *Damballah* as a novel. I've always thought of it as a coherent collection of interrelated short stories. *Fever,* of course, is a collection of short stories in the traditional sense of a collection. Is that correct?

WIDEMAN: I sort of thought that too, Charles, but I'm not so sure now. Because a lot of the stories were reworked and reorganized for the volume, and over half were new. And it doesn't have the kind of organic unity that *Damballah* had. But I'd like to think that the stories have unity in this sense. There's something really rotten in the state of Denmark. Something's really screwed. And the stories are ways of coping with the malaise which is in the air. "Fever," which is the final story in the book, attempts to render that essence, that unnameable uneasiness, that quality of decay or threat or collective anguish that permeates many of the other stories. Many of the other stories are about trouble, either people who are in trouble or who've fallen, and people who are working very hard to keep themselves from falling. And so the idea of the book, of the collection, is that this fever is amongst us still. This fever is something that we are subject to. Its ravages are still among us. So watch out folks. The final story in the book attempts to bridge, to synthesize past, present, and future sources of this fever, which to me clearly is the unresolved question of slavery, the unresolved question of racism, the unresolved question of majority rule that leads to majority domination and oppression.

ROWELL: I shall never forget seeing a photograph of you in an issue of *Sports Illustrated,* where you were standing before a chalkboard. On that board, you had written statements about Albert Murray. You've also written literary criticism about his work. You've also written about Zora Neale Hurston, about Charles Chesnutt, and about Gayle [*sic*] Jones. These writers are Southerners. Do you find something in them, artistically, in a positive way, that you don't find in other African-American writers? I'm thinking now about your interest in voice, in an article you wrote for the *American Poetry Review.* Voice, of course, is of primary importance in the elegant writing in *Damballah,* and in the texts which follow it.

WIDEMAN: I think there is such a thing as a core to Afro-American culture. There is a core culture. And part of it can be identified. And you can have fun talking about what you think the core is, but there is definitely one there. We'll never be able to define it once and for all, because then we'll probably start slipping into ideology rather than description. But there is a core and it has to do with the South. It has to do with the locus of that "letter from home" phrase you mentioned before. There was an understanding in me of Southern culture although I never ventured further south than Ohio until I was about 20 years old. As a kid I didn't know I was a carrier of Southern culture in Pittsburgh. My parents were not born in the South. You would have to go all the way back to my grandfathers, both of whom were born in the South. But indirect exposure to that core culture generated by the African background is enough to stamp us. It's what we all share. Knowing the deep structures of African-American culture can tell you more about people than knowing the part of the country that they come from.

ROWELL: Your work obviously indicates that you have studied different literary traditions. In fact, you talked about those traditions earlier in this interview. In terms of what you have set for yourself as a writer, as an artist, how do you view yourself in relation to other American writers, specifically African-American and European-American writers?

WIDEMAN: I like the idea of a writing community. And I'd like to feel myself a part of one. I'd like to feel that we are all in the same ballgame. I like that sense of respect, mutual respect, that you get when you go to the playground. When you go to the playground to play basketball there are no referees. And the game can't be played unless there is a certain degree of mutual respect and understanding about the rules. And I think it would be wonderful if we had that kind of community and that kind of mutual respect and understanding in this country, rather than cutthroat, commercialized competition and competitiveness. If the rewards were more evenly distributed, if we weren't all fighting the blockbuster syndrome, in which a piece of writing either goes to the top or gets no attention at all. If we had more good bookstores. If the literary establishment had a wider sense of what's valuable. If there weren't so many goddamned unexamined assumptions about what's good. If we taught writing and language more rationally, more humanely in schools, maybe this ideal sense of a literary heritage and a literary community would be a reality. Of course it isn't, and I guess I'm simply describing what it might be at its best and what I'd like to relate to and feel myself part of.

Home: An Interview
with John Edgar Wideman

LUSTIG: You moved from Homewood when you were twelve, yet it's the place that you keep circling back to. I find it interesting that, despite all those years away, it's the primary place in your work, that you keep going back to it as defining *home*. Maybe you could talk a little about that.

WIDEMAN: Okay, but let me start with distinction. There is a neighborhood in Pittsburgh called Homewood. It was there before I was born and probably when I'm dead it will still be called that. It's considered a number of streets, houses, population changes—people get old and die. It's a real place in that sense. Now, for many of the years between birth and about twelve, I lived in Homewood. Other times I've lived in Shadyside, which is a completely different neighborhood. That's the level of fact. The distinction I want to make is that, once I started to write, I was creating a place based partly on memories of the actual place I lived in, and partly on the exigencies or needs of the fiction I was creating. Once I began to write, to create, I felt no compunction to stay within the bounds of Homewood. Now how that fictional place relates to the actual Homewood is very problematic. And, depending on the questions you ask, that relationship will be important or irrelevant, superfluous.

If I were to tell the story of your life in my fiction, I might talk about your height, and keep you tall, but I also might make your hair dark, because I want a heroine who has dark hair. And I might know your parents well, or know just a tiny bit about them, but I could make one a sailor, and the other a college teacher, just because that's what I need in my fiction. People could then go back and say, well now, what did Wideman know about this young woman named Jessica, and how long did he

Jessica Lustig, "Home: An Interview with John Edgar Wideman," *African American Review* 26.3 (Fall 1992): 453–56. Used by permission of Jessica Lustig.

know her, and how tall is she really, and what do her parents do? But all that might or might not have anything to do with the particular book in which you appear. So although I have lived in other places, the Homewood which I make in my books has continued to grow and be confident. It has its own laws of accretion and growth and reality.

LUSTIG: What I think is really interesting about the way this Homewood, in your books, is figured is that the post-1970 landscape has been in a lot of ways devastated. Your characters—and you, for that matter—talk about Homewood Avenue as it is now, as opposed to what it was in the '50s, or the '40s. And yet the way in which the people relate to each other makes it feel almost like a rural place, like a small town. I think that a neighborhood is an urban construct, so I'm very interested in the way that these people seem to interrelate as a small-town community.

WIDEMAN: I go in the other direction. I think it's the people who make the neighborhood. That's the difference between learning about Homewood through my writing and learning about Homewood from sociologists. There have been interesting books written about Homewood, but the people make the place. They literally *make* it. Yes, Homewood Avenue is devastated, but when the character in "Solitary" walks down that street, she sees the street at various times in its history. So it's populated by the fish store, by five-and-tens. She remembers places that were there when she was a little girl. Characters do that all the time. They walk through the landscape which, from the point of view of some person who's either following them with a camera or looking at them from a distance, is just vacant lots, but the person in the story sees something else. What counts most is what the person inside the story sees. That's where the life proceeds; that's where Homewood has a definition.

In other places in my writing I talk about how the old people *made*, created the town. But they created it not so much with bricks and boards; a lot of them simply moved into houses where other people had lived. They created it through their sense of values and the way they treated one another, and the way they treated the place. That's *crucial* to the strength of Homewood, and it's something very basic about African-American culture. Africans couldn't bring African buildings, ecology, languages wholesale, in the material sense, to the New World. But they brought the invisible dimensions of their society, of our culture, to this land. That's what you have to recognize: This world that's carried around in people's heads overlays and transcends and transforms whatever the people happen to be. So it's not anything that people in Homewood invented. To make something from nothing is almost a tradition.

LUSTIG: I'd like to hear more about why it's Homewood, and not parts of Philadelphia, not parts of Laramie, that you write about. You've been in many places that you could write about as, figure as, home—many places in which you could absorb the stories. A lot of times it seems that your places are alive because of the stories that people tell about the places, continually, to keep them alive.

WIDEMAN: Well, there's something simple going on here. Those elements of Philadelphia that I came to appreciate and enjoy, and the same with Laramie, I plug into Homewood. They're in there, although they're kind of disguised. If I met somebody yesterday who had some quality that I felt was fascinating, and it either reminded me of my grandfather or suddenly opened up some mystery that I had in my mind, well, I might stick that in. It's not like there's this well of Homewood experiences that I keep drawing from; it's stuff in the future that I'm also locating there. It has to happen that way, or else the work would become static, a moldy thing, nostalgic. The neighborhood, the place, is an artistic contrivance for capturing *all* kinds of experience, and it works to the degree that it is permeable, that things that happen outside Homewood continue to grow up.

Part 3

THE CRITICS

Introduction

Wideman's short fiction has received surprisingly little critical attention given its generally positive reception by reviewers and its increasing presence in anthologies and course syllabi. In part, this may be a function of his versatility; his longer works of both fiction and semiautobiography lend themselves to extended commentary, especially on social issues. Moreover, since his first collection was part of a trilogy that included two novels, the stories are often read within the larger context rather than as distinct pieces. The criticism selected for inclusion here focuses on *Damballah* because that is the collection that has received virtually all the attention. Within that limitation, an attempt has been made to show a range of critical views.

James Coleman was the first to note Wideman's modernist sensibility and the ways that perspective shifted after his 1973 novel *The Lynchers*. This early phase, with its clear influences of James Joyce, T. S. Eliot, and William Faulkner, was followed by Wideman's struggle to place himself within African-American literary and cultural traditions. As Coleman reads his career, *Damballah* was one of the first products of that new vision. The passages selected develop the notion of the black intellectual seeking a way to engage the black community authentically.

Sven Birkerts reviews the collection retrospectively at the time of the reissue of the Homewood trilogy in 1992. He sees *Damballah* as central to an understanding of Wideman's vision, in that it reveals the writer's special talent as a "witness" to history and culture. He uses examples from several stories to show how Wideman creates the fabric of community and of his saga.

Ashraf Rushdy offers an interpretation of Wideman's narrative technique by focusing on the means by which the Other gains a voice in his fiction. In the Homewood writings, he sees this as occurring through letters, storytelling, and music, especially the blues. He argues that Wideman came to see that to presume to speak for the Other was an act of solipsism and exploitation. Therefore he sought ways to hear that transcended the self. The selection included here focuses on two stories from *Damballah*, "Reba Love Jackson" and "The Beginning of Homewood." In both cases, John, the narrator, moves beyond his own assumptions about what the story should be in order to understand it from a different perspective.

James W. Coleman

The most important thing Wideman does in *Damballah* . . . is to describe the black intellectual-writer's arduous movement back toward the black community and black culture. Wideman understands from his reading of other black writers and from his interaction in the community that the intellectual-writer is not necessarily an outsider, as he is often depicted in the mainstream modernist tradition. He also now fully understands that black culture is rich and substantive and that the black intellectual can both benefit from it and play a role in developing it. But the black intellectual has a problem because he has alienated himself, and he must master the culture and work himself back into it. Wideman goes further in *Damballah* than he did in *Hiding Place:* he speaks in a black voice that is even louder and stronger, and he shows a black intellectual, often identified as John and obviously a surrogate for Wideman, as he seeks to move out of isolation and to play a role in the black community. . . .

It is noteworthy that *Damballah*, although made up of individual pieces, has a unity often found in modern short-story collections that is associated with such mainstream modernist writers as James Joyce in *Dubliners* and William Faulkner in *Go Down, Moses* and also with such black writers as Ernest Gaines in *Bloodline* and Richard Wright in *Uncle Tom's Children*. *Damballah* has this unity because it largely uses a clear, well-defined setting, Homewood; because it presents central themes from different viewpoints; and because it depicts the development of an authorial attitude toward the setting and subject matter. This unity makes the book closer to a novel than to a collection of unrelated short pieces. In fact *Damballah* is formally very similar to Wideman's novels. Furthermore, in it, like other twentieth-century black writers, Wideman has used a mainstream modernist technique to present black themes. . . .

From James W. Coleman, *Blackness and Modernism: The Literary Career of John Edgar Wideman* (Jackson: University Press of Mississippi, 1989), 79–81, 95–96. ©University Press of Mississippi. Used by permission.

In *Damballah*, Wideman achieves a more uniform black voicing of contemporary and historical black problems than he did in *Hiding Place* and begins to shift back toward a focus on the black intellectual and his place in the black community. The characters are frequently speaking in their own folk voices, as in *Hiding Place*, but the difference is that the folk voices successfully project solutions to problems from the beginning and do not become bogged down in a mainstream modernist psychological alienation, as do Bess and Tommy in *Hiding Place*. In *Damballah*, Wideman is further from the stream-of-consciousness technique, with its internal focus, and is thus more removed from mainstream modernist form than he has ever been in his literary career.

The most thought-provoking aspect of *Damballah*, though, is Wideman's treatment of the intellectual quest. The intellectual-writer John is struggling for rapprochement with the black community and tries to project a voice deeply imbued with black cultural tradition. "The Beginning of Homewood" indicates that John has made great progress in his quest.

Sven Birkerts

Damballah is the linking element here. It is also, as it happens, the best place to begin reading the Wideman archive. For in these loosely linked narratives we not only meet the presiding figures of the author's imagination, but we also encounter in their first formulation the anecdotes and legends that will surface—fleshed out or told from other vantages—in the other books. Wideman is not an inventor. He has little of the fabulist in him and could never spin the kinds of webs that Morrison spins. He is, rather, a writer of very specific witness. He writes what he knows, and what he knows—the world bounded in his nutshell—is the family and kinship network of Pittsburgh's Homewood section. Homewood is a small place, a few dozen raggedy streets, but when seen with the historian's, or genealogist's optic and inhabited by a spirit of high empathetic susceptibility, it is place enough. Through his laminations of detail and his cunning manipulation of echoes, Wideman accomplishes for his Pittsburgh what William Kennedy has for his Albany: he fixes his place to the page as a permanent, and in many ways a universal, habitation.

"Damballah" is an ancient divinity, and as part of the epigraph citation (from Maya Deren's *Divine Horsemen: The Voodoo Gods of Haiti*) has it: "One song invoking Damballah requests that he 'Gather up the Family.' " Which is, in a sense, just what Wideman does, not only in this work but in his entire oeuvre. The complex family tree that he places before the text leaves no doubt that these are his own people, and that the stories, while allowing a few liberties, are true. What makes this work fiction is the author's way of burrowing into the identities of his various characters.

For Wideman, gathering the family does not mean setting out its extended tale in any chronological fashion. Quite the reverse: Wideman pursues the logic of intimate narration. That is, he stitches together the anecdotes from the family hoard, but does so as an insider would, dis-

From Sven Birkerts, "The Art of Memory," *The New Republic* (13 and 20 July, 1992): 43–44, 48–49. Excerpted by permission of *The New Republic*, ©1992, The New Republic, Inc.

pensing with explanatory transitions and cutting back and forth through time in a way that almost assumes familiarity with the big picture. If there is a density about Wideman's page, it has less to do with stylistic complexity—though he does write a packed and muscular prose—than with the reader's need to keep scrambling for a new space-time foothold.

Damballah is the source book, even though many of the characters and incidents will only take on their full significance later, as passages in other books reinscribe their centrality. Here we first read about John French and Freeda Hollinger, Wideman's grandparents, who married in the early 1900s and had four children, one of whom, Lizabeth, is the author's mother. "Lizabeth, The Caterpillar Story" recounts a key episode. Freeda sits rocking a young Lizabeth on her lap, telling her a story about a caterpillar, when she suddenly sees her husband coming along the alley. She also sees that the man behind him has pulled a gun. Freeda promptly crashes her fist through the windowpane, alerting John French to danger, and thereby earning the scar that becomes a kind of bead on the family rosary. While nothing overtly tragic has happened, the moment captures something essential about the family's life: the nimbus of danger that John French wears, the resourcefulness and domestic protectiveness that Freeda embodies. That afternoon takes its place as one of the essential tales in the family repertoire.

Lizabeth, as a girl, loves to sit in Freeda's lap, and loves to listen to her reminisce about early days in Homewood, the times when "Cassina Way nothing but dirt. Crab apple trees and pear trees grew where you see all them shacks." And Wideman in his turn loves to dizzy the reader with unexpected time switches, as in this parenthetical aside:

> Lizabeth needs her mother's voice to make things real. (Years later when she will have grandchildren of her own and her mother and father both long dead Lizabeth will still be trying to understand why sometimes it takes someone's voice to make things real. She will be sitting in a room and the room full of her children and grandchildren and everybody eating and talking and laughing but she will be staring down a dark tunnel and that dark, empty tunnel is her life . . .)

The cadences map the circlings and repetitions of intimate discourse; they gradually connect us with the indescribable potency that lies at the core of all family life.

If the focus of the early stories falls on John French and Freeda and Lizabeth, the later pieces bring a more distressing present into view. It is a tragedy in the life of the real Wideman family that Robby, the author's younger brother, was arrested in 1976 for his part in a robbery, a crime that left one man dead at the scene. Wideman gave the event full-length treatment in his *Brothers and Keepers,* but it has obviously haunted his fiction-writing imagination as well. Indeed, as Wideman wrote in that book:

> At about the time I was beginning to teach Afro-American literature at the University of Pennsylvania, back home on the streets of Pittsburgh Robby was living through the changes in black culture and consciousness I was reading about and discussing with my students in the quiet of the classroom. . . . I was trying to discover words to explain what was happening to black people. That my brother might have something to say about these matters never occurred to me.

By the time he wrote *Damballah,* however, he had discovered the words. In the story "Tommy," Wideman plants himself for the first time in his brother's shoes, summoning up the rage and confusion that spawned the crime and accompanied the terrified escape attempt. He pushes in past the Black Power slogans of the day to expose the look and feel of a changed world. What was once a rough but cohesive community is now, at least in Tommy's eyes, a ravaged place from which hope has been barred. Drugs and violence, familiar specters of our own day, tyrannize the streets. It is the most dizzying time switch of all, the bisection of the molten flow of memory by the jagged tremors of a new urban reality. Tommy has not been able to escape as his brother did. Homewood comes to us filtered through his sense of entrapment:

> It was a bitch in the world. Stone bitch. Feeling like Mister Tooth Decay crawling all sweaty out of the gray sheets. Mom could wash them every day, they still be gray. Like his underclothes. Like every mother fucking thing they had and would ever have. Doo Wah Diddy. The rake jerked three or four times through his bush. Left there as a decoration and weapon. You could fuck up a cat with those steel teeth. You could get the points sharp as needles. And draw it swift as Billy the Kid.

As *Damballah* reminds us Wideman may not be a master of the classic short story but he is a sublime storyteller. When he works in extended sequences, free from the demands of formal plot architecture, he is unexcelled. And this collection, my cavils aside, shows the writer working at full muscle, tunneling through the past to connect with the ore rifts of generational experience, but also exposing rifts of the other kind—the societal rifts that have defined so much about black culture in this country and elsewhere. Reading Wideman's collections presents us with a graph of atmospheric changes in black cultural life. Our job is to chalk the overlay graph, the one that shows the political and economic depredations by the powers that be. As Homewood has gone, so has gone the nation.

As I suggested at the outset, there has been for some years a vacancy at the table of African-American letters. In one sense, of course, it is nonsensical to speak in terms of "leading" this and "foremost" that. But we do it anyway. And while any number of black women writers have staked a claim to the distaff title, the males have not generated a similar excitement. We have no Ellisons, Wrights, or Baldwins in recent memory. Writers like Ishmael Reed, John A. Williams, Charles Johnson, David Bradley, and Al Young have all done vital work in fiction, but none has manifested that cumulative solidity—not yet—to make them inheritors of the mantle.

On the basis of the gathered evidence, I would say that John Edgar Wideman has. Though he has not sought the public spokesman's role, he has certainly been having his say. His depictions have evolved into an ever more comprehensive picture of black American life in our time, and they have done so sanely and empathetically. The work is balanced—humanly balanced—with extreme scenarios taking their place alongside the evocations of more prosaic domesticity. Through it all there is a feeling of life pushing on with unstemmed momentum.

Wideman may not be a writer bent upon positions and polemics. He feels too strongly the novelist's traditional piety before the workings of fate in individual lives. This does not mean, however, that he cannot get angered and righteous about the miasma of our racial relations. (*Philadelphia Fire* crackles with its narrator's rage at the hypocrisy and corruption of the white power structure.) But Wideman's vision charges him to make constant provision for love and goodness. The urge is toward inclusiveness and accommodation. He is building a picture of the world the hard way—person by person, life by life. He is now our leading black male writer and (casting the nonsense of these divisions aside) one of our very finest writers, period.

Ashraf H. A. Rushdy

The next two stories in [*Damballah*] begin to assume that telling is basic to all acts of narration, and they develop the distinction between two forms of using the voice: writing and singing. When he tries to write the stories, John finds himself appropriating the events he is recording: "I have written it before because I hear my mother now, like a person in a book or a story instructing me. I wrote it that way but it didn't happen that way." What happens when he writes is that the voices get lost: "When I wrote this before there was dialogue." Meanwhile the story of the gospel singer Reba Love Jackson teaches us how song transforms story into life in a way that writing is incapable of doing: "Couldn't speak about some things. She could only sing them. Put her stories in the songs she heard all her life so the songs became her stories." It is the empathy involved in "listening" that allows Reba Love Jackson's songs to be both part of her life and yet nonetheless representative of those lives about whom she sings. It is, in the end, her ability to listen that gives her songs their poignancy. At the beginning of the story, the narrator answers a phone call for Reba Love. Listening to a man tell of his troubles, the narrator feels somewhat embarrassed. He puts down the receiver and gets Reba Love on the phone. "I stood beside her while she listened. Seems like I understand better. Watching how Reba Love listened. How the face of that saint got sad-eyed while she shook her head from side to side. I'm hearing the man and understanding him better than when I was holding the phone my own self." Even though she is not singing, Reba Love, simply by listening, is able to express more effectively the blues of someone else's life.

Listening is, for Reba Love, an act of identification. . . . In a sense, Reba Love makes the songs of other people's lives hers by assuming selflessness, by relinquishing her ego in an act of listening. It is what John must learn—how to understand language and how to listen.

From Ashraf H. A. Rushdy, "Fraternal Blues: John Edgar Wideman's Homewood Trilogy," *Contemporary Literature* 32.3 (Fall 1991): 327–28. Reprinted by permission of the University of Wisconsin Press. ©Board of Regents of the University of Wisconsin System.

Part 3

By the final story of the collection, John learns. He had heard May's story, and Freeda's story, and Lizabeth's story, but he had found that writing transformed those stories by taking the voices out of them. In his final story, the one most explicitly epistolary (addressed directly to his brother Tommy, whose story preceded it), John reflects on the beginnings of Homewood—the escape of the slave Sybela Owens: "Her stories exist because of their parts and each part is a story worth telling, worth examining to find the stories it contains. What seems to ramble begins to cohere when the listener understands the process, understands that the voice seeks to recover everything, that the voice proclaims *nothing is lost*, that the listener is not passive but lives like everything else within the story." It is by learning to understand how voices exist and are transmitted that John finally learns how to be an active listener. The truly told story becomes that in which a listener inhabits the text. His letters, that is, find their ideal listener. Indeed, as he continues, John discovers himself occupying the place of griot, and this time he has an active audience: "Somebody shouts *Tell the truth*. You shout too. May is preaching and dances out between the shiny, butt-rubbed, wooden pews doing what she's been doing since the first morning somebody said *Freedom*. Freedom." Both May and "you" (and we must remember the way that pronoun was made ambiguous in the dedicatory letter) are quite literally part of an *audience*.

Chronology

1941   Born 14 July to Edgar and Betty French Wideman in Washington, D.C. Family soon moves to the Homewood neighborhood of Pittsburgh.

1951   Family moves to Shadyside, an upper-middle-class white community, where Wideman attends Liberty School and Shadyside High School.

1959–1963   Studies at University of Pennsylvania, majoring in psychology and English. Also is a basketball star.

1963–1966   Studies at Oxford University on Rhodes scholarship. Receives bachelor of philosophy degree.

1965   Marries Judith Ann Goldman.

1966–1967   Attends University of Iowa Creative Writing Workshop as Kent Fellow.

1967–1973   Faculty member of English Department at University of Pennsylvania. In 1972–1973, serves as chair of Afro-American Studies Department.

1967   *A Glance Away* is published.

1969   *Hurry Home.*

1973   *The Lynchers.*

1973–1986   Faculty member at University of Wyoming. Does not write for several years. Begins intensive study of African-American literature and culture, which leads to the 1981–1983 publication of the Homewood trilogy.

1975   Brother Robert is involved in a killing committed during a robbery and is eventually sentenced to life in prison without parole. The incident becomes the basis for several stories and for the book *Brothers and Keepers.*

1981   *Damballah* and *Hiding Place.*

1983   *Sent for You Yesterday,* which wins the 1984 P.E.N./ Faulkner Award for fiction.

1984   *Brothers and Keepers.*

1986   Takes teaching position at the University of Massachusetts. His son Jacob kills a friend while on a summer-camp trip to Arizona. Wideman deals with the tragedy in *Philadelphia Fire* and in various short stories.

1987   *Reuben.*

1989   *Fever.*

1990   *Philadelphia Fire,* which wins both the P.E.N./Faulkner and American Book Awards for 1991.

1992   *All Stories Are True* and *The Stories of John Edgar Wideman.*

1994   *Fatheralong.*

1996   *Cattle Killing.*

Selected Bibliography

Primary Sources

Short-Story Collections

Damballah. New York: Avon, 1981.
Fever. New York: Henry Holt, 1989.
All Stories Are True. New York: Vintage, 1992.
The Stories of John Edgar Wideman. New York: Pantheon, 1992.

Novels

A Glance Away. New York: Harcourt, Brace & World, 1967.
Hurry Home. New York: Harcourt, Brace & World, 1969.
The Lynchers. New York: Harcourt Brace Jovanovich, 1973.
Hiding Place. New York: Avon, 1981.
Sent for You Yesterday. New York: Avon, 1983.
Reuben. New York: Henry Holt, 1987.
Philadelphia Fire. New York: Henry Holt, 1990.
Cattle Killing. Boston: Houghton Mifflin, 1996.

Nonfiction

BOOKS

Brothers and Keepers. New York: Holt, Rinehart & Winston, 1984.
Fatheralong. New York: Pantheon, 1994.

PERIODICAL NONFICTION

"Frame and Dialect: The Evolution of the Black Voice in Fiction." *American Poetry Review* 5.5 (1976): 34–37.
"Defining the Black Voice in Fiction." *Black American Literature Forum* 2 (1977): 79–82.
"Of Love and Dust: A Reconsideration." *Callaloo* 6 (1978): 76–84.
"The Architectonics of Fiction." *Callaloo* 13 (1990): 42–46.

Secondary Sources

Interviews

O'Brien, John, ed. *Interviews with Black Writers*. New York: Liveright, 1973. 213–23.

Samuels, Wilfred D. "Going Home: A Conversation with John Edgar Wideman." *Callaloo* 6.1 (February 1983): 40–59.

Rowell, Charles H. "An Interview with John Edgar Wideman." *Callaloo* 13.1 (Winter 1990): 47–61.

Lustig, Jessica. "Home: An Interview with John Edgar Wideman." *African American Review* 26.3 (Fall 1992): 453–57.

Books and Parts of Books

Byerman, Keith E. "John Edgar Wideman." In *American Novelists Since World War II: Third Series. Dictionary of Literary Biography*. Vol. 143, 1994.

Coleman, James W. *Blackness and Modernism: The Literary Career of John Edgar Wideman*. Jackson: University Press of Mississippi, 1989.

Mbalia, Doreatha Drummond. *John Edgar Wideman: Reclaiming the African Personality*. Selinsgrove: Susquehanna University Press, 1995.

Journal Articles

Berben, Jacqueline. "Beyond Discourse: The Unspoken versus Words in the Fiction of John Edgar Wideman." *Callaloo* 8 (1985): 525–34.

Berben, Jacquie. "Towards a Black Realization of the Hegelian Ideal: John Edgar Wideman's 'Homewood.' " *Cycnos* 4 (1988): 43–48.

Rushdy, Ashraf H.A. "Fraternal Blues: John Edgar Wideman's Homewood Trilogy." *Contemporary Literature* 32 (1991): 312–45.

Clausen, Jan. "Native Fathers." *Kenyon Review* 14.2 (Spring 1992): 44–55.

Saunders, James Robert. "Exorcizing the Demons: John Edgar Wideman's Literary Response." *The Hollins Critic* 29.5 (December 1992): 1–10.

Index

The Author

Keith Byerman is professor of English and women's studies at Indiana State University and associate editor of *African American Review*. He is the author of *Fingering the Jagged Grain: Tradition and Form in Recent Black Fiction* (1986); *Alice Walker: An Annotated Bibliography*, with Erma Banks (1989); and *Seizing the Word: History, Art, and Life in the Work of W. E. B. Du Bois* (1994). He has published articles and reviews in *American Literature, American Literary History, American Literary Realism, CLA Journal, College Literature, Journal of American History*, and *Modern Fiction Studies*, as well as in several collections of essays.

The Editors

Gary Scharnhorst is professor of English at the University of New Mexico, coeditor of *American Literary Realism*, and editor in alternating years of *American Literary Scholarship: An Annual*. He is the author or editor of books about Horatio Alger Jr., Charlotte Perkins Gilman, Bret Harte, Nathaniel Hawthorne, Henry David Thoreau, and Mark Twain, and he has taught in Germany on Fulbright fellowships three times (1978–1979, 1985–1986, 1993). He is also the current president of the Western Literature Association and the Pacific Northwest American Studies Association.

Eric Haralson is assistant professor of English at the State University of New York at Stony Brook. He has published articles on American and English literature in such publications as *American Literature, Nineteenth-Century Literature*, the *Arizona Quarterly, American Literary Realism*, and the *Henry James Review*, as well as in several essay collections. He is also the editor of *The Garland Encyclopedia of American Nineteenth-Century Poetry*.